Create And Be Seen

A complete guide to Social Media Marketing

Written by Marlize Marais

First Published in 2021

Beyond The Vale Publishing

Contents

Introduction

Marketing is not everyone's core business and yet we need to market if we want new clients and generate a higher income. The amount of marketing you put in, is in direct correlation with the amount of money you will generate.

Over the past year I have done program after program after program to learn how to market on Social Media. What I have learned, I have customised and put into this book. My only goal with this book is to help other new entrepreneurs (or even if you're not so new), to make life easier.

After finishing my own planning and remaking the templates until I was happy with them, I realised that there are so many other people out there that will benefit from the templates as well. and thus, the idea for this book was born!

While you adjust the templates to suite your needs, always remember that the number one, most important thing you will ever need in marketing, is the mind!

The Mind

Social Media Marketers would like us to believe that having a software program to create our content or a planner for business strategies is the most important tool when it comes to social media marketing. I assure you, it's not. Of course, it is important to plan and have tools to make your life easier, but these things are not the most important. You can greatly benefit from a content planner and you cannot drive success in your business without a strategy or roadmap of how to get there. Yes, we must plan. However, planning still comes in second on my list of important things to do when it comes to social media marketing.

Keeping positive

At the very top of this list is the mind. More accurately, a positive state of mind. Without this first and most important thing that you must possess when it comes to social media marketing, all the other important things cannot happen successfully. You have to be motivated, and have desire and faith, for planning, strategy, creation, etc. to happen, not to mention happen successfully. It is our desire that drives us, and our faith that pushes us forward over the obstacles in our paths. Without the state of mind of desire and faith, you cannot plan your social media strategy and expect successful results.

We all think of ourselves in a certain way. You might think that you are hardworking and put in the necessary hours to accomplish a task. Another might think of himself as being lazy, hates himself for it daily, but stays true to his personality and gets truly little done. An older lady might think that she is far too outdated with technology and put in only half the effort as a result. These are three simple examples of the state that our minds can be in, and how it might affect the outcome of our success.

When I started creating my content planner to market this book, I searched through hundreds of podcasts, articles, and blogs. Every single one I came across explains why marketing on social media was so difficult. They tell a story of millions and millions of advertisers trying to catch the eye of the consumer. They describe the social media scene as overpopulated and overstimulating for both the mind and the eye. They mention great companies who have succeeded online with their marketing strategies and outline the role of all the employees involved to tap creativity from and how each keeps the ball rolling with their own area of expertise. By the end of my research to create my content for online marketing, I was terrified. I can't compete with that! I'm not a professional copywriter, I write stories! I have no background in marketing or advertising, and those people mentioned have degrees in this field. I am one person. I don't have a team to check my work and back me up.

For a while, I thought that social media marketing was too hard. It seemed like an impossible task to compete with people who have it all figured out. People who know the impact on potential consumers by using the exact right font and colour and image for posts and advertisements. When choosing an image for a post, I choose one that I like, not one that will have a phycological effect on a client! How am I supposed to know what will cause my potential client to stop their mindless scroll through the newsfeed to read my advert? As I focused on this fear, I couldn't write one post that made any sense. I looked at my planner and hated the little bit that I had done. I couldn't imagine someone reading a post and finding it interesting or worthwhile. And I stopped. I stopped all the planning and creating, the fear overwhelming me.

Your state of mind determines your outcome

I soon realised though, that I had been brainwashed. The truth is that you can speak to your perfect client with ease. Once you know exactly who you are marketing to, you will know how to market to them. With this realisation came peace of mind. I don't have to advertise like the rest of the world. I don't have to use their colours and tips and tricks. I am allowed to do this my way. I know who I am marketing to, and those people will see my adverts. The right people will be drawn in by my headliner because it interests them. They need what I have to offer. As my worries faded away, I was again able to focus on the value of my books, the clients I wanted to reach and the lives I wanted to touch, without fear paralysing me.

For further proof that your state of mind will determine your outcome, consider for a moment what a post will look like when someone focuses on the value they can offer, compared to someone desperate for money. The first post will be filled with passion, where the second post will seem needy. Think of the old fashioned, yet accurate belief, that you must smile when speaking to a client on the phone. Just like a friendly tone of voice can be conveyed through a telephone, when the listener can't see the speaker smile, a state of mind can be conveyed through an advertisement on social media.

A practical example

What kind of emotion do you feel when you see another weight loss advert with before and after pictures? Compare these emotions with what you might feel if you see a short video clip about how healthy your poop will be when you start with the new diet advertised. The logic behind it is that a healthy diet will make your whole body healthier, which will lead to all your organs and processes functioning at an optimal level, including the metabolic processes, leaving you with healthier poop than ever before. There are a thousand other benefits to using this diet, but the advertisers decided to focus on internal health instead of the mainstream "looking good" trend.

With the first example of the before and after pictures, you might feel irritated or indifferent because we have seen so many of these kinds of advertisements. If you've been on a diet before or used any dietary supplements, you might feel a little excited or disappointed depending on your results. But chances are, your emotions will be so unimpressed that you will forget ever seeing that advert within an hour, if not sooner.

With the second advert, however, something will stir. Whether you find this hilarious or embarrassing or even disgusting, it will be a stronger emotion than with the first advert, causing you to remember it better.

Now, what do you think the people creating these adverts were feeling when they were putting it all together? In the first example, the person was probably creating that advert out of habit. This is how we do it because this is how it has always been done, giving the advert little thought and emotion. Which in turn will be remarkably like what the consumer might experience. While creating the second advert, the advertiser was shifting his focus completely away from the norm, brainstorming new ideas, got to poop, and probably laughed out loud at this ridiculous idea to mention the word poop on social media. He ran with it anyway, creating excitement and anticipation for the reaction from the public, high levels of emotion also then experienced by the potential consumers.

These are two extreme examples of how the emotion you create an advert with will be experienced by the receiver. In our normal everyday lives, however, most of us sit down and think of planning and writing content as just another exercise to get through. Another task to tick off the to-do list. While I was in my state of terror for social media marketing, I didn't achieve much. I was only able to create content and advertisements of value once I've shifted my focus. The way you are feeling will not only affect the response to your adverts but also your input.

Shifting your focus
The key that unlocks all the above-mentioned emotions, is shifting your focus. Instead of focussing on the money that you need, that we all need to pay the bills at the end of the month, try tapping into the value of your product or service and the emotional relief that your client will feel once they have experienced what you have to offer. To accomplish this, you simply have to practice and be aware of your thoughts.

These two factors, practice and awareness, are the key ingredients to your success. No art can be mastered without practice and repetition, and that which controls us, the mind, cannot be controlled in turn if we are not aware of how it is controlling us. Once you understand the intricacies of the human mind, you will also understand that your thoughts lead to certain actions. You are not procrastinating because it is a part of your personality type or a nasty habit that you've formed, you're procrastinating because somewhere in the back of your mind there is a thought that is causing you to fear something, feel depressed or stress about something that you might not even be aware of. These negative emotions that you are feeling are causing the action you are taking. There is always an underlying thought, a belief, that drives us.

Beliefs

Unfortunately, these beliefs that we have can be either positive or negative. Beliefs are implanted into our minds by past experiences, other people's opinions, cultural practices, and other external influences like the media. A belief is very rarely something that we have decided for ourselves as being the truth.

A good example of a belief being implanted into the mind is when a young child is being told that he should stop singing because his voice sounds terrible. The mother expressing this statement might be irritated with work, life, or love. Her intention might be a moment of silence to collect her thoughts. In the child's mind, however, the thought of his voice sounding terrible will stick, and later in life, he will think it a personality trait to be too scared to speak up and be heard. He will think of himself as just another shy individual and feel most comfortable in the shadows where he doesn't have to use his voice.

An extreme example, but feelings of unworthiness and loneliness, lack of self-confidence and passion are all born the same way. This is even more true if a sentence was repeated when we were young, the adults in our lives not realising the life-long effect that their words can have. How can you possibly be successful when you doubt your every decision because of lack of self-confidence? If you are feeling unworthy or not good enough, do you think clients will jump on board with your services when these are the emotions that they are feeling from you?

The good news is that we as adults can now change all the negative beliefs about ourselves. We don't have to continue feeling lazy, inadequate, or shy, and believe that these are personality traits that our entire family were born with. You can remake your identity to what you want it to be. You can take the best qualities that you admire in others and embed them into your mind.

Before you do this, however, you need to eliminate as many negative beliefs as possible. We are ruled by our subconscious minds. No matter how positive our conscious thoughts might be, the negative beliefs in your subconscious will still determine your actions. You need to bring these beliefs to the surface and shine a light on them because only once you are aware of a belief, can you start changing it, and ultimately eliminate the thought altogether.

The most difficult challenge we face is finding these beliefs. The subconscious is a very dark, very deep, and extremely vast place. For this reason, I highly recommend that you continue with the exercise mentioned hereafter for the rest of your life. Even if you think you have eliminated all the negative beliefs stuck in your subconscious, there will always be more thoughts that get stuck because of continued outside influences.

Never stop challenging your beliefs. Always consider where they come from. Make your own decision about a topic. How do you feel about it? Or is what you believe a result of what society would like you to believe?

You have the answer

To investigate specific beliefs, you can use this rule: The subconscious will always answer every single question you ask of it. Be aware though that it is possible to ask your subconscious the wrong question. If, for example, someone was to ask themselves, and therefore their sub-conscious, why bad stuff was happening to them, their subconscious will find every possible answer relevant to their question.

Whether practical or not, and whether positive or not. This can range from "The world is a bad place" to "I have really bad luck", creating more negative thoughts and feelings. If this person instead asks how he can stop having bad things happen to him, his brain will react in the same way, because this is simply how the brain was built. Only this time, instead of unwanted reasons, it will take the how into consideration and give him ideas and strategies, all relevant to past experiences, personal and otherwise, to prevent having another bad day. Giving this person solutions instead of reasons and excuses.

Because of this complexity of the mind and running the risk of asking the wrong questions which might get you stuck on a negative train of thought or stuck in a negative state of mind, there is a simple exercise you can follow instead. Rather than ask yourself a question, ask your mind to fill-in-the-blank. This will provide much more specific responses, and you will be able to pinpoint negative beliefs regarding a certain topic.

I am

For a simple demonstration, start with the words "I am". You can write it down, say it out loud or think it consciously. Now listen. Your subconscious will complete the rest of the sentence. What is that little whisper in the back of your mind telling you? That you are strong, courageous, determined, successful and awesome? Or do you hear whispers of unworthiness, being lazy, scared, intimidated or even weak? You can replace the "I am" with absolutely anything to discover your true beliefs. "Money is", "work is", "my passion is", or even "I can", "I can't", "I should be" or "love is". Your subconscious will complete the sentence every time if you keep your conscious thoughts quiet for a couple of moments. Write it all down. Keep a list of all your beliefs, positive and negative.

This is where the work starts. This is the first step to success, and not, like society would like us to believe, creating a content planner. Discover and then alter your identity, your beliefs about yourself, into how you would like to show up in your business, and not how other people have made you believe that you should. Show up for your clients with confidence and passion. Show them that you care more about their results and the value of your product or service than what you can get out of it. The benefit of this kind of mindset is not only more money because of better results on advertisements, but also practising the art of giving. Selling your product or service yes, but doing so from a place of caring and helping others. Focussing on touching people's lives for the better, are much more satisfying to the soul than any amount of money ever received.

New beliefs

The most effective way to install new beliefs into the subconscious mind is by continuous repetition. If you have discovered thinking of yourself as unworthy, start repeating to yourself that you are worthy of every good thing coming your way and that you are ready to receive it. Repeat your new sentence, your new belief and affirmation in the first person, "I am". The most effective way I have discovered of repeating these affirmations is by recording them in my own voice.

Using an audio merging application on my phone, I've added background music and extended the track to thirty minutes. Most audio players also have a repeat function to listen to your affirmations over and over. I now listen to my own voice telling me that "I am strong", "I am successful" and "I can do anything", every morning when I apply makeup, wash the dishes, or water the garden.

The result of listening to these affirmations daily over a couple of months, is less self-doubt, tapping into the talent that is my passion to earn a living while helping others and no longer overwhelm when a difficult task comes up. The more you work with affirmations, the more your subconscious mind will start believing what you tell it, even if it doesn't agree at the beginning.

The truth is that the success of your business is determined by you, and you alone. What are you willing to do to make this happen? What is your "this" in the first place? What is success to you? What is your success? What is your end goal? Your ultimate, perfect future? How determined are you for your success? Have you decided yet, and are you willing to stick with it no matter what obstacles might temporarily block your path?

These questions, coupled with your beliefs, your identity, determine your success, not the words you use in an advertisement. Because the kind of words that you use will be determined by the state of mind that you are in. Your mind is the first step.

Have you ever considered how many people go through life accepting that they just are who they are? How many people stop for a moment to ask the question: "Who am I?" And how many of these people then really consider the answer? Because it's not who you are that is holding you back, it's who you think you are. Ask yourself the questions mentioned earlier, make sure you know where you are going before you get to how you can get there.

A clear vision
When you are ready, when you have a clear vision of where you are heading, you can move on to step number two: planning. This is the roadmap that will guide you to the success you now have in mind. While you work through the rest of the book to setup your plan, always continue with the exercises mentioned

here in this first chapter. For example, while working out your messaging sequence, keep your value in mind, your identity and how you would like to show up for your clients. The step-by-step guidelines in this book will only work if you combine them with your new attitude of success. Change what you must. Adapt the information and templates to align with your business and your identity. Put glitter on it if that's what it takes. Make this work for you.

And always, work on the state of your mind.

My Perfect Client

Here's a valuable marketing rule that will serve you well: If you speak to everyone, you speak to no one.

When it comes to planning, the first thing that you need to do for your business is sit down and figure out who you would like as a client. Who is that Perfect Client that you are marketing to?

If you have a business that is anything like mine, I personally feel that EVERYONE that uses social media as a marketing tool should be reading this book.

I've struggled with this concept for some time before I realised that it is perfectly ok to have more than one perfect client. The main reason to identify your perfect client is to address a specific person when posting or putting offers out there. For my books, I will for example create an advert or post and talk to new entrepreneurs specifically, or in another, a person struggling with the technical stuff on social media.

Remember to add emotions and feelings to your client's profile, since people buy the emotion and NOT the product. Or simply put, the relief, the joy, the excitement that they will feel once the purchase is done. They don't look at a product and think:

"Sure I can use this." Our brains immediately bring emotions into the purchase.

To help you along the way, I've created a template for you to identify your perfect client. Simply answer the questions listed in this chapter in as much detail as possible.

After completing this template, I promise you, your advertising and posting will change to more personal interaction, since you will know and understand your client so much better.

We will have a look at who the person is, tap into their emotions and have a look at where you can find them. It is possible to engage on a more personal level with your clients if your posts or advertisements are more specifically targeted in the direction of a specific person.

You can create Excel or Google Sheet templates as we go along, write your information out in a book, or type it out in a document format. Choose whatever option works for you, and where you will easily be able to find all the information that you've gathered. Your templates should be your guides, and easily accessible. Make your life as simple as possible.

For all the following chapters, I will give you my answers to all the questions, and my completed templates as examples, to get your mind going, your creative juices flowing and give you some ideas. For the purpose of this exercise, I will use one of my Perfect Clients: New Entrepreneurs that are overwhelmed by all the different aspects of creating his/her new business.

WHO IS YOUR CLIENT?

Step 1 – The Superficial Stuff

We will first have a look at the more superficial, more obvious things regarding your client.

Imagine sitting at a coffee table, or wherever you will be most comfortable, with your perfect client opposite to you. Imagine that this client is your super fan. He or she will buy every new product or service that you have to offer, because he or she believes in you and your product or service. This is your dream client.

Imagine specific things about your client and regarding your industry. For example, what is she wearing? Does she wear jewellery or carry a handbag? Does she have children?

You can take this exercise as far as you can, to get the exact image of the client that you would like to work with. What does this person need to have or not have to fit in with your product or service? Does your product or service provide only an emotional solution, or is it something physical that your client needs?

For lack of a better example, a Netflix salesman first needs his client to have a television. Make this as real as possible in your mind, to pinpoint the exact person that you will be marketing to.

Include as many physical attributes to your client as possible and add them to the list on the next page. The questions include my answers for my perfect client as an example.

17

How old is your client?
   40 – 60

What is your client's gender?
   Male or Female

What is you client's marital status?
   Not Applicable

Does your client have any experience or education?
   Not Applicable

What is your client's job title and what functions do they perform at work?
   New Entrepreneur / Marketing / Marketing Strategy

What industry is your client in?
   Any (Even though for each post/offer I will address a specific industry like crafters, personal growth, etc.)

Where do your client live or work? What region, country, or province?
   South Africa

Which languages does your client speak?
   English or Afrikaans

What do your client's finances look like?
   Not Applicable

Describe your client in one sentence.
   He or she is open to new opportunities / Up for a challenge

Step 2 – Digging Deeper

Imagine what kind of personality your client will have. What kind of personality type would you like to work with? Someone that is always serious, or more relaxed about work? Someone that is confident and courageous, or shy and unsure? No matter what kind of person you imagine sitting in front of you, he or she does exist. They are all waiting for you to change their lives. This is your duty, your obligation. The next questions to ask is:

What are your client's values?
   Trustworthy / Authentic / Hardworking / Driven / Friendly

What are his or her desires and/or needs?
   Drive sales / Get new clients / Simplify business strategies

Describe your client's average day (When Working)
   Work from home, positive attitude, a lot of client
   interaction, spend a lot of time on social media, also
   admin/general tasks, goal setting

Which basic human need are you addressing?
(Certainty / Significance / Connection / Growth)
   Certainty - uncomplicate business processes
   Connection - better interaction with clients
   Growth - growth in sales because of better connections
   with clients / learn how to manage social media
   Significance - grow his or her brand

Step 3 – Emotions

What are the frustrations and problems that they are experiencing **BEFORE** being introduced to your product or service? We are focussing on the problems, because we want to pinpoint how our product or service can help them.

What do his or her emotions look like? What state of mind is your client in?
Fear of failing online.
Frustration because of poor business processes.
Frustration or stress because they are struggling to get everything done.
Stress in general because of work, working with people, finding work/life balance.

Challenges
Connecting with clients online
Reaching targets/goals
Getting new clients
Creating adverts that are effective

Objections to sale
There's so much social media stuff out there, how will I know if this one will help me?
I've seen social media content planners; I still don't know how to get the ideas to populate them with content

Keeping your previous answers in mind, how will your client feel **AFTER** purchase?

Will his or her emotions change? How?

Relief and joy because this is a simple process to follow. Excitement about having clear business processes in place. Relief and joy because of stronger professional relationships.

How will your product or service solve his or her challenges?

Connect better with online clients
Get new clients (therefore sales) with ease

How can you ease his or her mind regarding their objections to the sale? What is in it for them?

This is an all-in-one template-based book, to get everything that you need for social media marketing in one place. Unlike most content planners, I show you how to create your own content planner with the content that needs to go into it

Can you save your ideal client time or money?

Money - don't lose clients (and money) because you don't know how to navigate social media marketing. You don't need to use paid advertising to make your advert work.
Time - simply fill in a template without spending hours trying to figure out what goes where and which elements to include and which not.

In the Content Creation chapter, I show you how you can compile ALL the pain points, objections and struggles for your different Perfect Clients into one place and use this to create valuable content when posting and advertising.

You now know exactly who the person is that you would like to sell your products or services to. All you need to remember, is to visualise this person sitting in front of you when you create an advertisement, a program or content for your social media feed.

In your mind's eye, chat to this person. Talk to him about his struggles and concerns and explain how you can help them. Explain your solution to his problem. By doing this, we also focus more on the problem and the solution, than on the monetary value that we get out of it.

Also keep in mind that some pain points are not things that people think about actively. For this reason, we always name the pain point in an advert. If you, for example, tell people about this amazing book with all these templates for social media, they might think: Oh, that's cool. But if you remind them first that they are struggling with social media marketing that thought will change to: I need this!

But more on advertising and posting in the following chapters. For now, keep your client's pain points in mind, to better know who it is that you should be talking to.

WHERE IS YOUR CLIENT?

You now know exactly who you want to talk to, how to address them according to their struggles and what they are currently experiencing without your service or product. But how do you find them?

Ask yourself the following questions:

What Groups will my client belong to?
Sales groups / Business Development / New Entrepreneurs

Which Hashtags will my client be following?
#businessdevelopment / #clientrelations / #sales / #onlinemarketing / #socialmediamarketing

What are Keywords that describe my client?
My client will have keywords like sales, social media, clients on his/her profile or posting or asking or searching for these topics

What kind of Activity (social media or otherwise) will my client participate in?
Active on social media / attend seminars or events (name them if you can) / who do they follow?

Join the groups, search the hashtags and keywords, and check out their activity. Identify your client, start commenting on their posts and ask questions. "Hang out" where your clients will "hang out" and engage.

No one said building a business isn't hard work, but once you've completed the templates and done the work, your communication with your client will be much clearer and more personal, addressing the emotions, and therefore the value that it will hold for your client.

In the Client Engagement chapter, we will take engagement with your client further, but I do fear that most people, especially advertisers, have lost the true purpose of social media platforms. This purpose is of course to connect with others.

Always create with value and connection in mind. Simply put, whatever kind of content you are creating, whether that is an advertisement, a post, website content or even a program, you will succeed if you put the monetary value of your product or service to the side, and only focus on the value that you can give your client, as well as the connection that you can build with your client.

Through value and connection, you will build trust. It is this trust that will be your most valuable marketing strategy. Word of mouth is still the best form of promoting your business.

The Perfect Profile

If you are using a social media platform to generate potential clients, always keep in mind that your personal profile will be a part of the process.

Make sure you don't post too many of those epic weekend parties or every photo you have of girls with low necklines on your personal profile.

You are of course welcome to post about your children, your dogs, your friends, share jokes and valuable content, but make sure that whatever you do on your personal profile is aligned with your hopes and dreams for your business. It's ok if clients get to know the personal you behind the business, but how much they get to know is entirely up to you!

Two marketing tips that will serve you well, are: A confused mind doesn't buy, and people buy from people.

Also keep in mind that your connections might be a couple of people that you know personally, but most connections you've never met in your life. Which is why you should turn your connections into potential clients.

View your personal page/profile as a part of your lead generation, and not only to entertain people you've never met. A good idea is to change your banner and/or profile picture every month or so. Every time you do, the new picture or banner will show in your newsfeed for all your connections (or potential customers) to see, together with a link that I will show you how to add. The link or CTA (call to action) being the reason for the exercise.

I will discuss how to use a message sequence in the Client Engagement chapter, to turn your connections into clients.

Please note that all the steps listed below can be applied to your personal page (which should now be a part of your lead generation) and on your business page you can add links to your banner and logo as well (Facebook profile setups only, other platforms do not have these functions).

The reason why a link in the banner is so important, is because if people visit your profile, they can see immediately what you do and where to click to subscribe or buy your products. There's no searching, no confusion. You are telling them clearly to "click here" to get your product or service before they get distracted by yesterday's post.

The steps listed below will guide you to set up a profile that will help you generate leads or even sales, without you having to explain to people how to get in touch and then buy your product. In essence, the profile setup eliminates the middleman.

You are welcome to have a look at my personal Facebook profile as you set up yours. The link to my page is: https://www.facebook.com/marlize.marais.393

Step 1 – The Banner

The banner is the first thing you see on someone's profile and should represent your business and the dreams you have for your business. In the world of technology that we now live in, your banner will be similar to the old-fashioned "First Impression".

You can create your entire banner in Canva and use UnSplash for high quality images to add to your banner. (See the Resources chapter for the links to various websites that will assist you.) Canva also gives you the exact dimensions for your banner, so that it's the correct size to import into Facebook. You can use contrast colours to catch the eye or a single image as focus point. Start with a template if you are struggling to come up with ideas, or simply search online for different eye-catching banners.

Make sure your banner looks appropriate on your mobile feed as well as, that all text is readable, and not only on your desktop. You might have to centre your text more and not spread it out across the entire banner. Most people use their mobiles for Facebook!

Also keep in mind that your profile picture will be in the centre at the bottom of your banner, so work around that.

For an upcoming event, you can even advertise it in your banner with a clear CTA to "Book Now!"

Important Elements that you should include are:

Eye-catching, NON-CONFUSING banner.

Busy banners are not recommended, because A CONFUSED MIND DOESN'T BUY. Use two pictures at most, with a background colour or simple pattern.

Headliner

Make sure your new potential clients can clearly see what you are offering. Mine, for example, encourages people to "Start Reading". You can also consider "Start Learning" for a program that you would like your clients to sign up to, "Get your free (Name your Product) today" or "Sign up for (whatever it is that you would like them to sign up for)".

Clear CTA (Call To Action button)

This "button" is simply a square image added with text writing over it ("GET IT NOW" or "CLICK HERE"), and not actually a "link button". The link we will add in the next step.

Add your business logo, slogan or a catchy phrase

Brand awareness starts here. The more people see your logo, the more they will start feeling comfortable with your brand. If you don't have a logo or slogan, like me, you can add a catchy phrase to explain to people about your product, service, or your passion.

Step 2 – Add A Link To Your Banner

Click on your banner

On the right-hand side, you will see an "edit" button

Click edit and add a short description that should align with the headliner on your banner, for example: Grab your free product here. I added a list of my books that are currently available.

Add the link to your sales page, Landing Page or website. In my industry, for example, I simply added the links to the website where my books can be purchased.

What will now happen is if someone clicks on your banner, or "the fake button", they will see on this page, on the right, the link that they can click and follow to their free product (or whatever you would like to add).

Please note that your CTA is the link. A CTA, or Call To Action, is a button that someone can click that will take them to a page or website to either "Learn more", or "Subscribe", "Sign-Up", "Book Now", etc. If you don't have any kind of link to add at the moment, mark this spot. I will show you how to create a simple Landing Page, which you can add as your CTA at a later stage. There is no reason why you shouldn't have a CTA. You can even link this to your Facebook business page, where your CTA will be to call on clients to "Like" your page.

Step 3 – Profile Picture

Do exactly the same thing with your profile picture, add a link on the left when you click on your profile picture.

Add a short description.

Keep in mind that for platforms like Facebook the trend is to use more informal pictures, whereas LinkedIn is considered to be more professional.

That being said, I've seen a new movement on LinkedIn where people are updating their profile pictures to show more of their authentic self. Instead of the "office, working girl", pictures are now showing a "relaxed, working-from-home mother". Don't be afraid of just being you!

Show your clients the person that you would like them to see, because people buy from people.

I feel it also worth mentioning that your profile picture will be the "Face" of your business. Keep this in mind more than what is trending and show people what your business looks like. Do you have a carpentry business, and you are always full of dust from sawing wood, with messy hear and safety glasses? Why not be this person on your page as well? Selling jewellery? Dress in your Sunday best and shower yourself with jewels for this picture! A ring on every finger!

Step 4 – Bio

A lot of people miss the Bio. Most people who do use the bio, use it to describe their life or views or a current situation in one sentence. If you have ever seen the words "Link in Bio", this is where you will find that link on a person's profile.

As social media marketers we can use the Bio to add a one-liner that will describe our business, advertise an upcoming event or program, or make a powerful statement. You can even add a recent achievement, award, or goal that you would like the public to get involved in.

The Bio is a great way of advertising because this is the first place on your profile where your link (CTA) will be visible, without having to click on anything.

Your Bio shows directly underneath your profile picture and banner.

Click Edit on your Bio.

Add a catchy phrase and again the link.

You can change this up monthly as well for all your friends or connections to see in your newsfeed. Edit your banner, profile picture and bio at intervals. Don't change everything in one day!

Step 5 - Intro

Your Intro or About section is located on the left, underneath your Bio.

Edit your "About" info. Now click "Update your information". Go through all the sections on the left and add whatever information you would like to.

If you have a business page, link this to your work. Under the work section type in the name of your business page and select your page from the drop-down list.

Add any links that you might have. Websites, Funnels, Landing Pages or in my case, the links to different book selling websites.

You don't have to put in your entire CV if it is not applicable anymore. Again, show your clients what you would like them to see.

Contact information is always a sensitive subject, and you should add yours at your own discretion. You don't have to feel obligated in any way to give the world your contact details if you prefer not to. Always be careful of social media and the information you share. Not only law-abiding citizens use social platforms.

Step 6 - Featured

Featured is located right underneath your Intro.

You can only post an image in this area. Again, simply click "Edit Featured" to add or remove images or photos.

Create a meme, again in Canva, that shows a summary of your services or products, how a client can get in touch with you, or any links.

You can also swop images around to promote different services, products, workshops, etc.

You can add up to 9 images or photos.

It is also important to note that these photos will be public. Even if you have security settings that allow only friends to see your photos or images, the images you add to your featured can be viewed by everyone.

Note: The Featured image is not as impressive on mobile as it is on a desktop, and I had to add it separately on my phone, but it's still a great way for people to see a cool image of a special event or your business in general.

Now you're all set!

When someone visits your profile, which I do surprisingly a lot to send messages and check out profiles before accepting Friend Requests, people will immediately be able to see clearly what you do, and more importantly, what they can do to join your program or buy your services with your clear CTA!

Not to mention all the action that will be happening on your newsfeed when changing your banner, picture, and bio.

You can do exactly the same with your banner and logo for your business page (add links and CTA's).

Content Creation

Most resources share a content planner or content ideas that look something like this:

	Week 1	Week 2	Week 3	Week 4
Mon	Share a tip	Post a case study	Host a #AMA	Share a win
Tue	Go behind the scenes	Go live	Fill in the blank	Share a meme
Wed	Share your favourite book	Share a sneak peek: coming soon	Create a long post with benefits	Tell people how to sign up
Thu	Ask a question	Share a Quote	Thank your fans	Share industry news
Fri	Create a Poll	Share an article	Tell people what you sell and why	Share a joke

And while this is all good and well, where do you find actual content to put into these posts? What do you write about?

What information will you share in your long posts, short posts, and what questions do you ask?

Another thing that is now pushed into society is that you MUST post every single day to keep your audience entertained. I disagree with this belief. Post 3 times a week, twice if you want to, but be consistent. Of course, the more you post the more interaction you will get, but don't make this rule your absolute truth and post nonsense when you run out of ideas. Personally, I would rather have my clients truly engaged in my content, than throw stuff out there just for the sake of posting. Rather post less, but post value.

A lot of work goes into content creation. But most of it is pre-planning. Once you have all your pre-planning done, the rest is easy to fill in.

This chapter will also help you put all your client's concerns or pain points, your solutions, valuable info about your industry and so much more, in one place to draw from later.

We are going to do a complete breakdown of your product or service that will also help you put your advertisements and programs together. You'll also be able to create copy for a website, know what you can offer for free and create a sales page or Funnel by simply copying and pasting if you are putting all the information into a spreadsheet (which I do recommend for this chapter).

This chapter takes a lot of thinking and exploring your mind, it's all the hard work behind writing everything in your business, but once you are done, you'll have an abundance of information to draw from!

GET ALL THE INFORMATION / PRE-PLANNING

The Headliners

We will be looking at each of the following headliners individually.

- Pain Point, Struggle, Concern and Objection
- Benefits/Solutions in general
- Benefits/Solutions specific to your product / service
- Who am I Talking to?
- Podcasts / TED Talks / Video Clips + URL
- Articles + URL
- Leaders in Your Industry / Science / Statistics
- Free Content
- Holidays and Other Special Days
- What else can I write about?
- Why am I doing this?

Again, you can add these headliners into a spreadsheet if you like or write it out by hand.

My examples are to get your own ideas flowing, but please keep in mind that you can change anything at any time to suit your business and personal preferences.

Step 1 - Pain Point, Struggle, Concern and Objection

Write down every pain point, struggle, and objection your client might have to the sale. List as many as you possibly can. Take your product/service and look at it from every possible angle. Remember to take feelings and emotions into consideration as well.

You can have a look at your Perfect Client Template, but you can now list even more pain points if possible. We're later going to specify who you are talking to, which of your Perfect Clients you will be addressing. I find that if you list everything you've already got from the Perfect Client Template, without naming the client, but think in a more general sense of your product or service, you are able to come up with even more objections or pain points.

Example:

- Struggle with social media in general
- Don't know how to put all the business or marketing processes in place
- Struggle to find content to post about
- Not sure how marketing on social media works
- Struggle to engage with clients online
- Struggle to market your product successfully
- Adverts are not as effective as you would like them to be
- Struggling to niche down or find the perfect client

Step 2 - Benefits / Solutions (General and Specific)

For each pain point listed, write down a benefit or solution next to it. Write down benefits or solutions specific to your product, and/or general benefits. You'll find that sometimes you only have a general benefit, sometimes one specific to your product, and sometimes both.

Example:

Struggle with social media in general

General: Social media is the best, easiest and cheapest way to reach individuals / there are 26.8 million Facebook users in South Africa
Specific: Step-by-step guides to help you make it easy / simplify social media without a hassle / time saving templates included

Don't know how to put all the business or marketing processes in place?

General: Every business should have processes and goals in place to achieve success (backed up by stats)
Specific: Step-by-step guides to help you make it easy / includes everything that you need to include for the marketing / streamline your marketing with these simple processes

Step 3 - Who Am I Talking To?

This step will help you create posts to address a specific person with a specific concern. This is applicable to posting and advertising. Use your now completed Perfect Client Template, and simply list all of your identified clients.

Look at each pain point and decide which one of your perfect clients will be the best fit, who will struggle with a specific pain point?

Example:

Struggle with social media in general
People from the older generations that struggle with social media.
People struggling with technical stuff.

Don't know how to put all the business or marketing processes in place
New Entrepreneurs.

Struggle to find content to post about
Small business owners that market on social media.
New Entrepreneurs.
Business owners that struggle to get their marketing processes together.

Step 4 - Podcasts / TED Talks / Video Clips

Use keywords to search on YouTube or Google. For this book it would be things like marketing tips, client generation, social media, content, etc.

Finding podcasts and TED talks on your topic will not only be an easy share to your page but might also teach you a thing or two! Make sure to listen or watch the entire video to make sure it's relevant to what you do. In your post when you share the clip, add a summary in text of the video for those who don't want to sit through the whole thing. But also try to share clips that are not too long, I always go for no more than 10 minutes, but 3 minutes would be better. The shorter the better.

You can also add your personal view to a post instead of a summary if you prefer. Remember, people buy from people. The more your clients get to know the "you" behind the business, the better for building up trust. The professional "you" if you prefer.

This section works best if you do have a spreadsheet, since you can then copy and paste the URL of the video for later use. But make sure you have the name of the video (and the speaker if there is one) to find it again.

Example:

My social media strategy EXPOSED (Instagram vs. YouTube vs. Podcast) https://www.youtube.com/watch?v=T4ooCcl2kfw

Step 5 - Articles

To search for articles or blogs, type in a specific topic that you are looking for. For example: Social Media Hacks or The Psychology behind Selling on Social Media.

You don't have to search specifically for an article, since most articles online are blogs. (If you include the word "article" in your search, you get very different results. I find it's better to search in general and not include "article" in the search bar.)

Do the same as with the videos, add a summary or your personal view in the post when sharing an article/blog.

You can work through the posts, blogs, articles and websites, and include the ones you like. Again, remember to add the URL to find it again later on.

Example:

New Social Media Hacks You Need to Start Using Today
https://neilpatel.com/blog/social-media-hacks/

10 Ways Small Businesses can Improve their Social Media Presence
https://digitalmarketinginstitute.com/blog/10-ways-small-businesses-can-improve-their-social-media-presence

Step 6 - Leaders in Your Industry / Science / Statistics

This might take a bit of searching, but chances are there is someone in your specific industry that is dominating the field, has a million followers and always talks sense.

Listen to their podcasts, read their articles, create quotes that you find impactful, use the words: according to science / leaders in my industry found... when posting.

Statistics also make for a good post. It's easier to convince people of facts when you have something backing up your claims.

You can use this information in different forms in posts or advertisements. You can share a podcast from an industry leader, share a quote, an article about the science behind your product or put the stats into your own words and create a long post or one with bullet points.

Whatever information you decide to use under this headliner, make sure to populate your template so that you can easily get to the information you want to share.

Example:

Simon Sinek - "Communication is not about speaking what we think. Communication is about ensuring others hear what we mean."

Step 7 - Free Content

Your next step is to sit and figure out what small part of your business you can offer for free.

Maybe you can share valuable knowledge, a small service or even a product. You can also consider "How To" guides, free video lessons or a masterclass, a program that you create, one-on-one calls, or PDFs with valuable information.

Maybe join in a fun day somewhere, print your logo on bookmarks to hand out at bookshops, host a small breakfast if your budget will allow it, or offer your clients a free book for the first 10 clients that sign up.

Dive into your creative mind for this one. Search free gift ideas online but remember that this is a part of your marketing strategy for social media and should therefore preferably be something that you can exchange for an email address. Even if you don't get an email address though, you will build trust and connection with your clients.

Please note that this is not a bonus for an offer i.e., get 30% off, but rather something that you can give your clients to promote your product/service absolutely free.

Example:

- 6 Months' worth of Content for your Calendar
- My Perfect Client Template
- One-on-One call for a limited time (1 Day Special) for people who bought the book

Step 8 - Holidays and Other Special Days

Make a list of all the holidays and remember to add the dates so that you don't miss them!

Here is a list of suggestions or examples you can add next to every date. This is simply to keep the planning going, we are going to populate the actual content later.

And of course, if you can think of something else, go for it!

- Offer
- Free product/service
- Quotation
- Meme (Image only)
- My Personal View (Why I love celebrating this holiday)
- Question (For example: How are you celebrating? What's your view of this holiday?)
- Article (About this holiday)
- Video Clip (About this holiday)

Example:

1 May: Workers' Day - Free Offer, today only
16 June: Youth Day - Meme
18 June: International Picnic Day - My Personal View (Too many people don't celebrate this day)

Step 9 - What else can I write about?

When advertising, we don't want to go too broad with our topics, you want, after all, to advertise your specific product/service. But when you post, you need to be able to warm up and entertain your audience with topics relevant to your core business.

For example, even though I won't put an advertisement out there for the below listed topics, I can post about it and help people see the bigger picture. My core business being social media simplified, I can also chat about: Inspiration and motivation and time management.

These topics have nothing to do with my book, but as an entrepreneur you might like to read posts with these topics as well.

Another good example that I recently came across is that of a bike shop. They post about bike trails for after you've purchased a bicycle.

Don't sell every time you post. Think outside the box. Go back to your Perfect Client Template and see what else your client might be interested in. If you can keep it close to your core business, that would be even better.

Example:

- Inspiration and motivation for entrepreneurs
- Time management

Step 10 - Why am I doing this?

Dig deep in this section. Find your big WHY.

- Why am I doing this?
- Why am I so passionate about helping others?
- What is the big picture, my goals, my dreams?
- What do I see in the future for this product?
- What is my background?
- How did I come to this place?
- What drives me, inspires and motivates me?
- How do I get my work done?
- What are my processes?
- What resources am I using to ensure success?
- What are my successes?
- What have I failed in and how did I get back up from that?

Answer all of these questions, and you'll have a lot to write about! And again: people buy from people. Don't be afraid to share how you do what you do and why. People love reading other people's stories.

Example:

Why am I doing this?
Because of my own struggle with social media marketing. I know how long it takes to figure all of this out by yourself. And I know how expensive the courses are to attend.

Step 11 – Sequence

Consider one of your pain points / objections and create a series to put all the concerns to rest. For videos, typical marketing videos shouldn't be more than 2 minutes, 1 minute if you can.

Since we are now addressing a specific problem, make sure your audience has a clear CTA (call to action) in the form of a link or a button that they can press to sign-up, learn more, or so on. (More about CTA later) Create more than 1 sequence if you can, to create content for more than 1 month.

When you record yourself addressing the problem, start powerful, to grab the client's attention.

You can also add in your video or your post that you will be posting about this topic again next week, or the topic for this month every Friday, so that people can look out for your next video post.

Example:

Pain Point:

I don't know what to post / I don't have enough content to populate the planner that I downloaded.

Name of sequence:
All about content

Post/Video # 1:
What is content marketing? (Post 1 of 4)

- Focus on the client 100%, take sales out of it.
- What can you give your client? What's in it for them?

Post/Video # 2:
Where do you get ideas from for content? (Post 2 of 4)

- You have to sit and brainstorm this
- These are some examples (mention things from my Content Creation Chapter)

Post/Video # 3:
Once you have your content, what are you going to do with it? (Post 3 of 4)

- Think about where you are posting, and how
- Are you speaking this person's language, relating to them?

Post/Video # 4:
Measure! (Post 4 of 4)

- See what works, recycle your content
- If you think you have great content, with bad results, reword or use a different image

You don't have to have 4 videos or posts on a topic specifically, every single thing about marketing is applying it to your business and feeling comfortable and aligned with your goals and dreams with everything you put out there. Start with 2 videos or posts if you feel more comfortable with that. On the other hand, publish a video or go live with a specific topic every Friday (for example). That's also a sequence and you can follow the same structure to plan this.

I would recommend that you stick to one pain point for a certain period of time, so that all concerns regarding this one topic can be clarified. But no more than 6 times on 1 topic, otherwise it gets boring.

I already mentioned that it works great if you can create more than one sequence while you're working on this part of the planner. You already have all your pain points listed. Choose a few and add your solutions or benefits to them.

You can now have a look at your sequences and decide which ones you would like to make into a video sequence and which ones you are going to keep in a text format.

You can bring science or podcasts into it and talk about those topics for a while. But not for too long. Be careful of a Magic Monday or Wacky Wednesday or whatever, it tends to get boring after a while. The posts are always on the same monotone. Switch up your topics, keep your information fresh. If your content is valuable enough and you let people know more about this topic is coming, they will definitely be on the lookout for your other posts.

Step 12 – Write an Article

The last thing you can do is to write an article. Before you freak out, remember that you now have ALL the info, and once again you can simply use a template to put your article together. Simply fill in your answers next to the following headings:

Topic:

Name/ Headline:

Personal Background / What do I have to do with it:
    Why are you doing this?
    What's your passion?

Topic Background:

Who am I talking to:

Pain Points:
    How do they feel? Think about emotions

Solutions / Benefits:
    What will they have gained after purchase?
    How will you solve their problem?
    Can you save them time and/or money?

Pros and cons:
Science:
Leaders in your industry:
My product / My thoughts:
    What makes you unique?

CREATE YOUR PLAN

All your pre-planning is now done! When you are ready, you can start creating your actual content calendar. This table will serve as your Monthly Template. Create a table that looks something like this:

	Week 1	Week 2	Week 3	Week 4
Monday				
Tuesday				
Wednesday				
Thursday				
Friday				

Decide how many days per week you are going to post and which days. Stick to it. Like I've mentioned before, if you don't have enough GOOD content to post every day, rather post less. As long as you are consistent.

You can create two of these tables and use a different one every month. But you are welcome to use just one as well, very few people are going to remember what type of post you posted on what day.

You are also welcome to add Saturday and Sunday to your table. Remember, you don't have to physically sit in front of the computer to post, you can schedule them, over the weekends especially.

We are first going to have a look at the different types of posts that you would like to post. You can choose any of the following or create your own (I think I got it all covered though), and add them randomly into your table:

- List (Bullets) (No Image)
- Long text (No image)
- Text and image
- Text and video
- Meme (Image only)
- Share an article
- Share a podcast / clip
- Ask a question / Explain reasoning
- One liner
- Series
- Live
- Pre-recorded video
- Poll
- Fill in the blank (In the comments)
- Jokes
- Quotes
- AMA - Ask me anything
- Coming Soon
- Shoutout
- Share resources
- FAQ - Frequently asked questions

These are all the different posts that you can create on social media. Use the ones that you feel most comfortable with.

Example:

	Week 1	Week 2	Week 3	Week 4
Monday	One liner	Ask a question / Explain reasoning	List (Bullets)	Poll
Tuesday	Series	Series	Series	Series
Wednesday	Share a video clip	Meme	Jokes	FAQ
Thursday	Text and image	One liner	Fill in the blank	List (Bullets)
Friday	Share an article	Meme	Quotes	Long text
Saturday	Long text	Share a resource	List (Bullets)	Meme
Sunday	Pre-recorded video	Text and image	Shoutout	Quotes

There are enough types to add one to every day. You can of course use a certain type of post again: 2 or 3 memes, 2 long or list posts, etc. The content will be different for every post, even if you have 2 list posts included for the month or a week.

The idea of this step is to create your baseline, your template from which you will be working from.

Example 2:

	Week 1	*Week 2*	*Week 3*	*Week 4*
Monday	List (Bullets)	Meme	Share a video clip	Text and image
Tuesday	Jokes	Share an article	List (Bullets)	Poll
Wednesday	Text and image	Meme	Long text	Fill in the blank
Thursday	Share a resource	List (Bullets)	Quotes	Share a video clip
Friday	Series	Series	Series	Series
Saturday	Quotes	Meme	List (Bullets)	Text and image
Sunday	Long text	Text and image	One liner	Meme

Stay true to who you are. Go back to the first chapter if necessary and remind yourself of your goals, dreams and desires while working on this chapter. If you are scared to death of recording a video of yourself, ask yourself why? Is it something that you have come to believe about yourself because of other people's opinions?

Remember, in the words of Henry Ford and Tony Robbins: "If you do what you have always done, you will get what you have always gotten."

Now, have a look at the following list. You can add any of these to your table if you like to know exactly how you are going to start a post, especially the text posts. Switch it up however you like for each month or you can even stick to the same thing. Like I said, very few people are going to recognise a pattern from one month to the next. Add your own "Post Starters" if you've seen something that caught your eye. Complete your Monthly Template as far as possible before you start writing the actual content that needs to go into it.

- Calling out all...
- How we achieved...
- Do's and Don'ts
- Ever considered...?
- Checklist
- How to...
- 5 Ways to...
- 5 Tips for...
- Did you know...?
- Confronted by... I think...
- Why you need...
- ....makes me think/feel...
- As a business professional...
- Do you struggle with...?
- The Secret of...
- When someone tells you....I feel...
- The shortcut / cheat sheet for...
- I would love to hear your thoughts...
- Something personal about yourself...

- Your gift today...
- Pros and Cons
- Inspiration
- Challenge

Example:

	Week 1	Week 2	Week 3	Week 4
Mo	One liner **Did you Know?**	Question **Ever Considered**	List **5 Tips**	Poll
Tu	Series	Series	Series	Series
We	Video clip	Meme	Jokes	FAQ
Th	Text and image **The Secret**	One liner	Fill in the blank	List **Why you need...**
Fr	Share an article	Meme	Quotes	Long text **Inspiration**
Sa	Long text Pros and Cons	Share a resource	List 6 Reasons	Meme
Su	Pre-recorded video	Text and image Personal	Shoutout	Quotes

The series is already planned, so I don't need to include anything here.

I also only include the "Post Starters" from the previous page for the text posts that I will need to write out beforehand.
For an article (for example) I will switch it up between:

- I saw this article and thought it was really interesting...
- Check out this cool article that will help you...
- What an amazing article about...
- If you struggle with...this article is a must read!

Be Creative!!!
Let your imagination guide you!!!

You've now got your baseline, your template, all you need to do now is look at the information / data that you've already collected and populate the rest of the template.

Before you do that though, here are some general tips for posting:

- Use hashtags to optimise engagement:

  For Facebook hashtags, if you use:
11 #'s	-	79,5% engagement
9 #'s	-	49,5% engagement
5 #'s	-	43% engagement
2 #'s	-	41% engagement
8 #'s	-	39,5% engagement

  LinkedIn: Max 5 #'s, add 3 more when you share.

- The more engagement you have on a post, the more it is shared in newsfeeds. You can share a link in the comments, an extra idea or ask people to engage here in the comments and share their thoughts. Yes, comment on your own post to get the engagement up. You can also share your own post for the same reason.

- Ask your audience to turn their notifications on for your group or follow certain hashtags to keep receiving all the cool content. Use an announcement or the about section for this request.

- Like I mentioned before, be consistent. Whether you post 1 or 5 times per week, just make sure you stick to that EVERY week.

- The general accepted posting for putting offers out there is about 3:1. Meaning, post general info/content two times and make an offer/advertise on the 3rd post. When making an offer, make sure you have a clear CTA (call to action.)

- REMEMBER:
  The amount of offers you make is in direct correlation with the number of clients you will get! If you don't make offers, you won't get clients!!! That being said, if you sell on every post, people will get bored or even irritated. Share some cool info in between.

- CTA - your call to action on offers/advertisements should be very clear: a confused mind doesn't buy! Your CTA can be a button to press (usually sign-up / learn more / register here / book now) OR you can simply add a link to your post, keeping in mind to use your comments to boost engagement. For example, write in your copy/post: link is in the comments.

- Make sure you have contact details on EVERY SINGLE post. Whether that be a phone number, an email, a website address, a link to your Landing Page, or even just your logo. When your post is shared by others, people should know where the post is coming from. You can also add this in the comments.

- Make it as simple as possible. Again, a confused mind doesn't buy! Keep your content easy and clear and make it easy for clients to get in touch with you.

- Once you have everything set, you can add scheduled posts to your page/ profile, so that you don't have to sit in front of social media and post every day. Scheduled posting will make life so much easier for you, knowing that your Facebook page is running for the month, without you having to give too much attention to posting, since you've already done the work. BUT...

- Reply to EVERY comment that you receive, even if it is just liking the comment. Engage with your potential clients as much as possible.

- IMPORTANT:
  Facebook will block you if you post too many times in the same groups, rather share your posts from your personal or business page. And switch up the groups where you can post.

  They will also block you if you use too many of the same words over and over again. Keep every single post unique!

- TEST! TEST! TEST! Rerun advertisements and posts that have received a lot of engagement. Post again about this topic. Have a look at the image that you used, try it again with different text. Popular post types change weekly according to statistics. Don't get stuck with one or two types, try different ones, and see how your specific audience responds.

- Social platforms change monthly. Today there is a function that you loved, and tomorrow it might be gone. Click buttons, search online, ask friends or in a group, but don't fear social media. Chances are, you won't break it.

- ALWAYS write your content from your heart, from your soul and your passion. Emotions are contagious. Go back to the first chapter as often as you need to or make notes to easy access the exercises that works for you. ALWAYS work on your state of mind!

CREATE YOUR ACTUAL CONTENT CALENDAR

A content calendar works best in a spreadsheet. You are welcome to draw lines in a book as well, but keep in mind that the following information will be best suited for another table. There are also a lot that you can copy and paste once you've done the work so that you don't have to type everything out again. The headings run horizontally over the sheet, and I populate the info downwards.

I will break the headings into sections, and again give you examples of each for better explanation.

The first heading that you need to address is:

- **Day**

- **Date** - Remember to have a look at holidays or other special days

- **Goal** - Post / Offer / Free Offer

- **Type** - Use the previous table to populate this column (You can copy and paste from the previous table if you have it all typed out).

Day	Date	Goal	Type
Wednesday	4 Nov	Offer	Series
Thursday	5 Nov	Post	Poll
Friday	6 Nov	Post	Share an article
Saturday	7 Nov	Offer	Long text - Inspiration

- **Pain Point** - Choose any of your pain points or concerns that you've listed previously. For articles, podcasts and so on, leave this column open.

- **Topic** - Again using the previous table, but now add for example: 5 Ways to Create Content. Use the pain point from the previous column and your "Post Starters" to give your post a name.

This will be the headliner for your post. When creating posts in the multitude and on one day, I don't usually run all the headlines through the Headline Analyser (Link in Resources). Personally, I use the Analyser mostly for advertisements.

You can choose whether you would like to use or post your headliners or post names in this column. I have posts that I name, just to remember which ones they are, but don't serve as a headliner. Not all posts need to have headliners.

Pain Point	Topic
Struggle to find content to post about	All about content #1
Struggle to get business processes in place	Do you have a clear marketing plan? (Yes / No / Working on it)
	3 Ways to Use Psychology in Your Social Media Marketing
It's hard work to start a business	My Garden / Comparison

- **Content** - I like to pre-write all my posts in Google Docs or Word and then just write DONE in this column. I copy and paste from Google docs into my post.

Also check out UniCode Text Converter in the Resources, you can Bold or Italic your headliners on this website, and it stays that way when you copy it into the post.

Or if it's going to be just short text with a meme or quote or my series, I'll write the exact text that I want to post in this column and copy and paste it into the post from here.

Content
All about content #1 Here's the first of four videos that will explain everything you need to know about content! I've included a Link in the comments for you to check out the book with COMPLETE instructions to help you get started with your content planner. The link will take you to Amazon.com where all my books are listed. (Offer)
A business can only thrive when you have a clear set of goals and processes in place to reach those goals. Do you have all your marketing processes in place? POLL - Yes / No / Working on it
Done - Summary of Article in Docs
Done - Long text in Docs

An example of my Summary Article that I've pre-written in a document:

Hey guys!

This is a really cool article by Shane Barker on the psychology behind marketing.

Here's a summary for you, but they do explain in the article the why and how!

#1: Give Gifts to Encourage Responses
- Answer the question (for your client): What's in it for me?

#2: Use Emotional Triggers to Create Authentic Connections
- Establish a face and personality for your business
- Use laughter or empathy

#3: Partner with Trusted Authorities to Build Credibility
- To build trust with your clients, associate with brands they already trust

I would love to hear your thoughts in the comments!

Have an incredible day!
Marlize

An example of my Long Text, pre-written in a document:

I was watering the garden this morning and saw a bud on my little orange rose for the first time since last year.

I replanted this rose first from a pot into the garden, then my wall was rebuilt and had to take all the plants out to save them. This rose was standing in another pot for 2 weeks before I was able to again plant it out into the garden.

After I planted it in the garden the first time, it took a long time for the roots to settle, and just as it did, I had to take it out again for the wall.

But now, with the wall fixed and all the flowers back in the soil, it's finally showing its first rose in over a year!

I realised when I saw this flower that this is exactly what happened to my business. I had to rebuild a couple of times, go back to the drawing board, and revise my goals and my game plan. Brand awareness took some time, but now my work is finally starting to grow and show its first flowers.

Every time I now see that rose, I feel so calm, it will bloom with time. I did my best to take care of it, just like I do with my work, always ALL IN, and now, I can breathe.

What can you compare your business to that will help you see the beauty and growth in it and help you to stay calm? Share with us in the comments...

You are welcome to check out my book on social media if you are at a loss to answer this question. It includes EVERYTHING you need to help you get your marketing processes in place, so that your business can start blooming as well: (LINK TO AMAZON) (Offer)

Note: There is a character limit on all social media posts. You can easily search the web and find out what they are if you would like to plan accordingly. For Facebook, the limit is 63,206 characters.

- **Hashtags** - Keeping the number of Hashtags in mind as shown previously

- **Image** - or None

- **CTA** - The link or button or just say none. Applicable for all posts that are offers. (According to your Goal)

Hashtags	Image	CTA
#socialmedia #sales #content	Pre-recorded video	Yes - link to Amazon in comments
#onlinemarkerketing #entrepreneurship #businessowner	None	None
#entrepreneurship #customerrelations #sales	None - Link to article	None
#inspiration #businessowner #socialmedia		Yes - link to Amazon in post

I include the picture of the rose, even though it is a long post and not a text and image post, just to show you how complete the planning can be.

If you search all your images before the day of posting, and include them here, posting will become a breeze for you. I know exactly what I am posting on what day and EVERYTHING that I need to include in that post. No more trying to figure out what to post about this week or next month or giving yourself a headache because of the worry that goes with finding content to post about.

I have advertisements that run separately from my posting (offers) as well. But you are welcome to include your adverts as a part of your content schedule if you like. And yes, for these adverts there is a formula or template that I follow, as discussed in the Create an Advert Chapter.

For a very long time, I was actually scared of putting adverts or offers out there, because:

- There are too many advertisers on Facebook
- People scroll by your advert without even noticing it
- My copy isn't good enough to draw their attention
- My imaging and videos are not good enough compared to other advertisers

STOP COMPARING YOURSELF WITH ANYONE!

I didn't have a fear of promoting or what people will think of me (all brain drama), but I did have this fear of not being good enough.
I promise you, if you keep on posting from your heart and your passion and focus on the value of your product or service, instead of "I hope people sign-up" or "I hope people see my adverts", the right people will sign-up.

Of course, not everyone is interested in social media marketing, of course some people would rather find other solutions than reading through an entire book, of course people are going to miss my adverts because they don't hang out on social media the whole day.

But for those that do see my adverts and my posts, I will put all my creativity into it and make them understand what the value is for them. I will make my content clear and explain to them the problem and how I can solve it. I will help them see how I can help them, because this is my passion: Writing about things that I have experienced myself and helping others with everything I have learned.

Because Heavens only know, the struggle is real. I went through it, through all the tears of trying to market online and figuring out what to do next and how to reach my audience and what the hell am I posting again today!

When you write these posts and create this planner, stop all thoughts of money that are eating at your brain, and focus only on how you can help your audience. What is your value that you are offering?

Your thoughts make all the difference in the world!

- Where am I posting - For example Business Page, Personal Page, List the Groups you are going to share to from your business or personal page or group. List the groups that you can post in directly.

  Some groups have rules that allows you to only post on a Monday and a Wednesday for example. Make sure you know all the group rules for posting when using a community or advertising group.

  I've mentioned before that Facebook will block you if you post in a group too many times, that counts for sharing as well, but they are more lenient when sharing. But be careful, all social media platforms are sensitive to repetition. Rather share once a week if you're not sure. Take your best post from the week, the one that has received the most engagement, and share that post to a couple of places.

Where am I posting?
Business Page / Personal Page Groups: Benoni/Boksburg… / Midstream/Centurion/ Rustenburg
Business Page / Personal Page Groups: Potchefstroom / A-Z Centurion / Advertise Faerie Glen
Business Page Groups: Ek is vd Ooste / Northwest / Midstream Estates

- Engagement - After a week or so, add what type of engagement you received from this post. You can update the engagement every week if you like.

  You can then track the posts that had high engagement levels, reword them, add a new image, and post those again.

  You can see exactly how many people viewed your posts on your business page, as well as how many clicks there were if you included a link. Interactions include likes and comments.

  One of the things that makes it to the important list when it comes to marketing, is tracking your progress. In fact, tracking your progress is important for everything you do in life. You cannot grow, and learn, and adjust if you have not had a look at your results. Tweak what you have to. If you really like a post, but it has received low engagement, try a different image with it next time.

There's still a lot of guess work when it comes to posting, so test, test, test!

Engagement
People Reached: 357 / Shares: 4 / Interaction: 14 / Link clicks: 23
People Reached: 1432 / Shares: 7 / Interaction: 35
People Reached: 109 / Shares: 3 / Interaction: 2

You now have a COMPLETE content planner, with all the content that should go into it. It's hard work and takes time to get everything in place, but once you have this, I guarantee you, you will be thankful for the work you've put into it.

It takes all the confusion and worrying about what to post out of the equation!

After going through this exercise, you'll realise how much there actually is to post about. And what is more, you will have a complete breakdown of everything about your product or services in one place. All the pain points, solutions, statistics, science, articles, etc.

Whenever I need to create any kind of content for my business, I draw from this template.

Because at the end of the day, all business is, is finding a problem and solving it. If you can find a problem that a lot of people have and solve it for them, you have a business. There really is nothing more to it.

Now all you have to do is let those people know that you have the solution they have been looking for.

I think a lot of entrepreneurs overcomplicate things (everything) because there are so many things to learn and so many steps to take before you can be successful.

Keep it as simple as you possibly can! (Which is also the reason for these simple templates. Even though all of this might overwhelm you before you get started, it's still an easy process to follow!)

SCHEDULE A POST

You can schedule a post in Facebook from your business page or group. For LinkedIn, you have to use an external application to schedule posts. None of these applications, however, has a free option to make it worth your while.

Please do not make the mistake to think that scheduling a post takes all the social media maintenance out of the equation. You still have to manually share posts that you would like to share and respond manually to all comments received on a post.

In fact, I have found that I prefer to take some time every day and rather post manually. By doing this, you don't miss anything important happening on your pages or groups. When posts are scheduled, it's very easy to push social marketing to the back of your mind, and not attend to the task at all.

My advice, if you are not active on social media the whole day, is to select an hour each day, and make sure you post, respond, and share what you need to. If you are using only social media as your marketing strategy, see this time as part of your business processes, something that just must happen every day.

Scheduling on a Facebook Business Page

- There are two different options. One for a computer and one for a mobile. I prefer a computer for this work and will run through the computer sequence in full.

- If you work from your mobile, download the app called: Facebook Business Suite. Click publish, write your post, click next and then Publishing Options to schedule your post.

- For a computer: click "Publishing Tools" on the left on your business page.

- Again, on your left, click "Scheduled Posts".

- Then "Create Post" at the top.

- Create your post.

- Click the arrow next to "Publish" and click "Schedule Post".

- Select your date and time (keeping in mind when your Perfect Client might be most active on social media).

- Click "Schedule".

- You will notice "Publish" has now changed to "Schedule Post", click this button at the bottom of the box and done!

- You can view all your scheduled posts in this same section.

- To change a post or reschedule it, simply click on the relevant post, and change whatever you like.

Scheduling on a Facebook Group

- For a computer: Make sure you are in your Group on the homepage where you can see your newsfeed.

- Click "What's on your mind, ..." to create a new post (As though you would create a new post right now).

- Create your post.

- Click the Clock Button at the bottom of the box, right next to "Post" OR find a Calendar button.

  (Facebook changes things around very often, some of you might still see the Clock button, while others will need to search for a Calendar button that will specify "Schedule Post". They roll out changes or updates to a certain group of people first to test it, so not everyone's profile might look the same.)

- Select a time and date (Again keeping in mind when your Perfect Client will be most active on social media).

- Click "Schedule".

- And done!

- To edit or view your scheduled posts, click "Admin Tools" OR "Publishing Tools" on the left.

- Click "Scheduled Posts".

- Click the 3 dots OR the standard Settings button next to the post you want to edit.

- You can edit, delete, reschedule or "Post Now" your post from here.

IN SUMMARY – Let's break it down

1. Do the once-off work:

- Pain Points, Struggle, Concern and Objection
- Benefits/Solutions in general
- Benefits/Solutions specific to your product / service
- Who am I Talking to?
- Podcasts / TED Talks / Video Clips & URL
- Articles & URL
- Leaders in Your Industry / Science / Statistics
- Free Content
- Holidays and Other Special Days
- What else can I write about?
- Why am I doing this?
- Create Sequences
- Write an Article

2. Create your monthly template to work from every month.

3. Create a new table to complete the FULL planning. You can plan your content 3, 6 or even 12 months ahead. This table is the only one that you will actively be working on from month to month to create new posts.

4. Post it or schedule it!

And that's it!

You're all done and can now take a breath!

Congratulations!

The work after this will be much easier and go 10 times faster. For the rest of the templates, refer back to this one to work on a specific problem and include your solution.

Remember: the more you populate these tables, the easier the work will be in the future. (My list of pain points goes well into the 40s!)

"Don't use social media to impress people; use it to impact people." - Dave Willis

Content Creation

Create an Advert

I hope that by this point, I have repeated enough that you should be creating from your own authentic self and that you no longer think social media and the advertisements that goes with it is a difficult task.

Yes, we still have to look at the images that catch the eye, the headliners that are catchy and the content that is moving, but all in all, go with your gut. Go with your gut, your passion, your instinct, your desires, and identity, but also test, test, test!

There really is nothing more to advertising online, than being in the correct state of mind and testing. Not one advertiser, no matter how experienced they are, knows with absolute certainty what the response to an advert will be if they do not test the market first. And all markets are different.

Here, more than with any other exercise, chat to that Perfect Client that you have created in your mind. Choose a pain point and talk to your imaginary client about it. Sit with your Perfect Client template next to you, while creating your adverts. Tap into their emotions.

Because remember, we are not selling a product or service, but rather the emotion that it will bring to your client after purchase.

Before we start…

- Create 1 advert and track the engagement.

- Now run the same advert twice more, for each time change 1 thing about your advert and track the engagement. This way, you actively test the copy and the image or video. TEST! TEST! TEST!

- Use only 1 pain point per advert.

- An advert is different from a post, in the sense that you have a clear offer and CTA (call to action).

- Re-post advertisements that have done well according to their engagement rate.

- The average click rate on Facebook advertisements are   2 - 5% (Simply take the amount of clicks you've received on an advert (that is how many times your CTA button or link was clicked), divided by the number of people that have seen your post (post reached) and multiply it by 100. For example: an advert gets 54 link clicks and has reached 3400 people: 54 / 3400 x 100 = 1.5%)

- That being said, South Africans are old school, and our ratings are lower than other countries.

- For paid Facebook ads, you can download the Facebook Ads Manager in the Play Store and track your advert's progress.

ADVERTISING PLANNING

First have a look at the planning for your advert. You can create a new table, or write out the following information:

- Niche (Perfect Client)
- Goal
- Paid / Free
- Recurring
- Duration / Post Dates
- Where
- Number of Adverts
- CTA
- Funnel
- Email Action

Niche - Simply pick one of your Perfect Clients. Who do you want to talk to today?

Goal - Why are you creating this advert? Would you like clients to buy something or sign-up for a program? Other goals might be brand awareness, inviting people to follow your business page, visit your website, click on your Funnel, generate email addresses, etc.

Paid / Free - Not if the product or service that you are offering is free or paid, but will this advert be a free or paid advert? Paid adverts are run through Facebook's Paid Advertising Services.

Recurring - Is this an advert that you can post again? Or is it an offer for a special occasion like Heritage Day?

Duration/ Post Dates - You can run your advert for as long as you like. If you create 3 adverts, you can post them all on the same day in different groups. Or create 1 advert with slight changes to each one (copy or image) and see which 1 of the 3 gets the most responses.

I personally don't like posting the same advert in a group twice, but if you use this advert and change something, you can post it again in that same group.

If you create 1 advert, and change it 3 times, you can post it for 3 days in the same group, plus your business page, plus your personal page. That gives you a total of 5 days for 1 advert.

If you have 3 adverts using the same offer, and do the same with each one, you can post for 15 days, each time with something different.

For paid advertisements, you select the number of days your advert will be running for, and it stays the same for that period of time, coming up in different personal news feeds, and not on repeat to the same people.

It is sometimes difficult to fight the urge to change it before the time has run out if the advert is receiving a below average engagement rate but changing it will delay the process since it needs to be approved every time you change it. It's best to wait till it's done, then change it, run it again, and track the engagement.

Where - ALWAYS post your adverts on your business page or group for your current audience to see. You can also post the advert or share it to your personal profile. Join groups where you are allowed to advertise, according to area, work criteria or however else you identified your Perfect Client. SHARE your post from your business page into these groups, instead of creating a new post in a group, so that you can track the engagement on your business page. Underneath each post on your business page, you will see the engagement.

Number of Adverts - As previously discussed, I will usually create 3 adverts focussing on the same pain point and therefore offer.

CTA - A MUST IN ALL ADVERTS! If you can't tell your clients how to buy or sign-up (a clear press this button / follow this link) then they won't buy or sign-up. Very few people are going to message you or go search for a website if you just include a telephone number or website address. Make sure there is some kind of immediate action they can take. Adding a button or link to Messenger is also a clear CTA for them to get more info. They can just click the button and ask for more info, without having to copy and paste your telephone number or website address. Make it easy for your clients to get in touch with you!

Funnel - I include this step so that you can make sure your Funnel is set up and working if you would like to use one. And also, so that you can plan your advert in full, which goes with setting up a Funnel if need be.

Email Action - When you run an advert, you can use an automated process to send out emails to clients. You can either do this by using a Landing Page or a Funnel. I will explain more about automation in a following chapter. For now, answer this question: how are your clients receiving the product or service that you offer in the advertisement?

If it is something like a program that they are signing up to, you need to send an email to confirm the time and date, as well as include a link where they can join you for the program (if it's an online program). If they are buying something like an eBook, they need to receive the link to download the file they have purchased.

I recommend you read all about automation before setting up your first advert, unless you have a website where you can sell what you are selling while keeping the process simple.

That being said, don't rely solely on automation. Make it easy for your clients to interact with you, maybe ask a question to start a conversation in the comments, interact as much as possible, especially with adverts. Don't think you are just posting an offer, think in terms of getting your clients engaged with your offer!

"It's a dialogue, not a monologue, and some people don't understand that. Social media is more like a telephone than a television." - Amy Jo Martin

Example:

Niche:

New Entrepreneurs

Goal:

Sale / Buy this book / Clicks on the Amazon link

Paid / Free:

Free

Recurring:

Yes

Duration/ Post Dates:

15 Days: 5 - 20 Oct

Where:

Day 1: Business page, Personal profile, Groups: East Rand & Centurion Buy and Sell & Fourways (I will now plan this out for the next 15 days, making sure to rotate my 3 adverts, and the Re-Run of all 3 of them. This column will look the same for all 3 adverts that I am creating)

Number of Adverts:

3

CTA:

Link in copy and button underneath advert with "Learn more".

Funnel:

No

Email Action:

No

BUILD YOUR ADVERT

The next headings to address to create the advert are:

- Type
- Pain Point
- Solution
- Headliner
- Big Promise
- Guarantee
- Copy
- Image / Video
- Results / Engagement

Type - Go back and have a look at the type of posts that you can create on social media. Will this be a text and image post, a list or bullet post, a video post, etc? Videos tend to do better on Facebook, whereas list posts with bullets got the most engagement on LinkedIn. (For this week anyway!) The statistics around the most popular types of posts according to social media platforms really does change from week to week, so all you need to do is: TEST! TEST! TEST!

Pain Point - Focus on only 1 pain point per advert. You can repeat the focus on this 1 pain point for however many adverts you like to and add a different solution to it every time! Most of my pain points have at least 3 solutions for each one. Or use the same solution but change the type of post, the content and so on. Refer to your content planner if you can't remember!

Solution - Again, just have a look at all the work you already did in your content planner. Depending on the type of post you are using, you can either include only 1 solution (for example if you ask a question or state your opinion) or you can list a bunch of solutions (for example in a list or bullet post).

Headliner - Write down at least 10 headliners (20 if you can!) and run them through the Headliner Analyzer. The example that I'm using scored 66% (A link for the Headliner Analyser is included in the Resources section at the end of the book).

Big Promise - Think about it like this, you should be able to write your Headliner: And Big Promise after the colon! Even though you don't have to write it like this, you can also include your Big Promise in the copy / content of your advert. The Big Promise is to help describe your product or service better and promise the value that the client will be receiving.

Guarantee - For a free product or service that you are offering, you don't have to include a guarantee. Or you can attach a guarantee with no value to it, like in my example. This is more for paid services or products. People feel more at ease if they know they can get their money back for example, if you don't deliver the value promised. Or, if you have a product, you can offer the standard 1-year or 2-year guarantee on the product. You can put a time limitation or something that will qualify your client for the guarantee on it. Use something that you are comfortable with, that will put your client's mind at ease to buy your product or service.

Copy - Write the actual copy that will be in your post under this section. You can use the UniCode Text Converter to highlight your heading or other important elements in your copy.

Have a clear CTA for clients to take immediate action. If you have a button at the bottom of your advert, still include the link somewhere in the copy as well.

Remember to focus on your pain point and solution/s!

Image / Video - You can download high quality images from UnSplash. Or record your own video. Your marketing videos should be short and sweet, 2 minutes max.

You can use Canva to add text or images to your video. Your video plays, while the audience can still see the important "frozen" details at the side, bottom or top. Simply import your video into a Canva template, and design it however you like.

Results / Engagement - Track your engagement or results for every advert! Compare them, and use the ones with the highest engagement again, tweaking them as you go along.

Remember to not be hasty with this, give your hard work a certain amount of time before you decide whether it was successful or not.

A good tip: Don't delete or throw away anything that doesn't work. Keep EVERYTHING that your mind comes up with! This is the easiest way to track what works and what doesn't. But also, you never know what you might want to refer back to in the future, after learning and growing!

Example:

ADVERT 1

Type:
Text and Image

Pain Point:
Don't have all the social media marketing process in place

Solution:
Step-by-Step Guide to get you going

Headliner:
Social Media Strategy for New Entrepreneurs

Big Promise:
Take all the planning out of social media strategies, I've done that all for you!

Guarantee:
Headache free guaranteed, step-by-step guides

Copy:
(This is the actual post that I can now copy and paste)

Social Media Strategy for New Entrepreneurs
Who doesn't love templates? Simply fill in the easy-to-use templates and get your online business going without all the struggles.

Content Creation - Create the actual content, not just a calendar

My Perfect Client - Narrow down your niche, and talk to your dream client

Client Engagement - A complete, done-for-you messaging sequence

How to create an Advert - Includes all the important elements to build an advertisement

Building a Program - Use a program to get more clients

Take all the planning out of social media strategies, I've done that all for you!
Now available in a book format, to receive all the info you need to get going, in one place – (LINK)

Image / Video:

Results / Engagement:
  1.2%

You now have all the elements to post your advert. Do exactly the same to create more adverts, maybe try a video instead of an image for your second advert, or a meme instead for the third...

Re-run your advertisement and track the engagement:

RE-RUN 1 (ADVERT 1)

What am I changing?
Change the image to a short video: Marketing Video Clip 4

Results / Engagement: 2.1%

RE-RUN 2 (ADVERT 1)

What am I changing?
Keep the video clip, change the headliner to: Step-by-step guides to give your social media marketing a boost!

Results / Engagement: 1.7%

PAID ADVERTISEMENTS

Paid advertisements on LinkedIn are really not worth it. You'll get more engagement on your posts or offers if you run it through your normal newsfeed and business page.

LinkedIn, more than Facebook, has a thing referred to as "The Golden Hour". Within the first hour of posting a post, LinkedIn track engagement on it. If you receive any engagement on the post within that first hour, the LinkedIn algorithm will keep showing your post in other people's newsfeed. If, however, you don't have any engagements within this first hour, your post gets sent to the back of the line where it goes to die. Which is why on LinkedIn, more than Facebook, it's important to comment on your own posts and share them if you can.

Paid advertisements on Facebook, however, really are worth it. You can budget for as little as R 200 per month!

Paid adverts on Facebook can ONLY be run through your business page. You can't run a paid advertisement through a group. But you can of course copy and paste this advert into your group for that audience as well.

Remember that you must maintain every group and page that you create, which makes this extra work. You have to have a business page for paid advertising, even though most of your posting and engagement happens in the group. You are welcome to post only once a week to your business page if this is the case. Create scheduled posts for this purpose, and check engagement every now and then, but don't try to actively run both the group and the page if not necessary.

Because yes, marketing will lead to the results in sales, but marketing is still not your core business. Everything in this book is extra work. It's the behind-the-scenes stuff to keep the wheels turning, but not the actual business that you are conducting. Which is exactly the reason for writing this book in the first place. We have so many other responsibilities when it comes to business, your marketing should be something that runs smoothly and easily in the background.

Of course, I understand that you might be thinking at this point that the exercises here will keep you busy all day, but it's truly not so. Once you've done the pre-planning, once-off work, the templates will actually help you to save time on your marketing strategies.

You have 2 options for paid advertisements on Facebook:

1. You can simply create a new post on your business page and BOOST it.

2. OR you can click the "Ad Centre" option and "Create ad". If you choose this option, the advert will not be on your Business page's news feed, which is why I prefer Option 1. By posting the advert on the page first, your current audience (everyone that Like or Follow your page) will see the advert as well. Where Option 2 only shows your advert to a new audience that you create.

Option 1
(Both options work the same way if you choose to rather go with option 2)

- Underneath each post that you create on your Business page, you will see a button "Boost Post" - Click this button.

- You can now add a button to your advert / post - choose any of the options from the drop-down menu.

- Add a URL / link where the button should take the person that has clicked the button. For example: Funnel sales page, Landing Page or website.

- The next step is to create your audience - select gender, age, location and then add all the interests and demographics of your ideal client.

- Select the duration that you would like your advert to run.

- And the total amount that you would like to spend on this advert.

- Add your Credit Card details.

- Click "Boost post now" and you're running a "Sponsored" Advert on Facebook!!!

The process is really simple once you've created your advert from the above template, and you can now track how many people your post is reaching and all the engagement on the post.

You do exactly the same for the second option. The advert creation pop-up page looks the same.

You can work your advertisements into your content calendar if you like and boost the advert from your newsfeed.

Build a Program

Knowing how to build a program is a valuable skill in marketing. Programs can be used to generate new leads, for brand exposure and to give your existing audience an awesome free gift.

Building a program doesn't have to be difficult and complicated, it can be paid or free, hosted live or with pre-recorded videos and can run over 2 days or 20. You can even create a program for an hour webinar session if you'd like.

The most important aspect of building a program is to have a look at your specific needs for your business and decide on a goal. Would you like to generate more leads, or create a sustainable training course? What are the aspects in your industry that people might need more information on? What part of your business can you put into a program?

Let's look at something like a bike shop. What possible programs can they set up to generate more leads? (And I'll be thumb-sucking now, because all I know about bikes is how to put the chain back on my little girl's bicycle! But I want to use this example to show you how even the most unlikely type of industry can use programs to generate leads).

So how about:

- A pre-exercise program to warm up before you get on the bicycle

- How to properly care for / clean your bicycle

- Simple tips and tricks for when something breaks (boosting sales, because chances are, you're going to need special tools)

- Road safety when bicycling

- How to help your little one get started

(Ok, this is pretty much where my imagination stops when it comes to cycling!)

There are 5 ideas, if a bicycle shop owner jumps online and offers these programs for free using a sales page or Landing Page, he will not only expose his business to many more people but get email addresses as well. Email addresses that can then be used to keep clients updated on new products, launches, events, reminders, and so on.

Programs also help clients put a face behind the business, creating more personal interaction, because people buy from people. Instead of just running an advert on Facebook that says: "Visit our shop today!"

Here's an easy template that you can just fill in, to help you set up all the necessary elements for creating your program...

PROGRAM PLANNING

First have a look at the planning for your program. Note that this is very similar to creating an advert.

- Program Dates
- Niche
- Goal
- Paid/Free
- Recurring
- Where/How
- How many people can attend?
- Time
- CTA
- Email Action

You can fill in these answers after you've created your program (next template) if you would like to get clear on what it is that you will be doing, and how long it's going to take you.

I fill this one in halfway first and then build my program according to my availability. Because you can't move on to the next section if you don't know your Niche and Goal.

I move back and forth between the two tables. But please use these templates as you like, to make it easier for yourself.

Program Dates - You can run a live program over 1 or 5 days or record a video beforehand and run your program for an unlimited time. Include the launch date for pre-recorded videos.

Niche - Select one of your Perfect Clients.

Goal - Sign-up for free program / Increase shop visits / Drive website traffic / Follow my business page / Grow email list / Sales / etc.

Paid/Free - Webinars and pre-recorded videos will typically be free. A training program that runs over 2 - 5 days can be a paid program. Make sure you know what your goal is, and which type of program will suit that goal the best. For marketing, I would recommend a free program that won't take up too much of your time. Paid programs are a great way to offer extra value for already existing clients.

Recurring - Some programs might be a once off thing, for example a special for a specific holiday, leading up to an event, etc. Recurring programs will keep new clients flowing in, especially if you are using a Funnel and emails to make this process automatic.

Where/How - You can use pre-recorded videos, Zoom live, Facebook live, Google Meets or Webinar software. Make sure to test the program that you will be using and know how to share meeting links and so on.

How many people can attend? - For lives, make sure what the cap is on the software you'll be using. For example, the Free version of Zoom caps you at 40 min and only a certain number of people can attend. As far as I'm aware Google Meets have now changed to unlimited participants for unlimited time, but you might not be able to record the session.

Do your homework though, and make sure you don't get cut off in the middle of a live session!

Time - If you want to go live, plan this in your schedule and write down the times - for example Tuesday at 19h00 - 20h00.
CTA - This is not an option. You must have either a 'sign-up' button or a link that people can click on to join your program.

Email Action - Using email automation can help you deliver pre-recorded videos to your client's inbox. It can also send reminders for live training and include the link they should follow to join.

I recommend filling in this section as far as you can, before moving on to the next section. Leave whatever you don't know yet, design your program and come back to the rest of the planning.

Start with something simple, you don't have to have a complex program running, especially if this is your first program. Pre-recorded videos are an easy way to start!

Example:

Program Dates:
　　Launch 1 Nov

Niche:
　　People from the older generations that struggle with social media/ People struggling with technical stuff

Goal:
Generate more clients to buy the book, by signing up for free program (Marketing)

Paid / Free:
Free

Recurring:
Yes, I can re-run this program as much as I like
Where / How:
Pre-recorded videos

How many people can attend?
Unlimited - Pre-recordings will be delivered to the client's inbox

Time:
30 Minute video

CTA:
Yes, sign up button - linked to Funnel sales page

Email Action:
Yes = Welcome email + Video recording + How & Why to buy the full book = 3 emails

BUILD YOUR PROGRAM

Here are the next headings that we are going to be looking at:

- Duration
- Pain point
- Solution
- Name
- Big Promise
- Modules
- Bonuses
- Module Breakdown
- Bonus Breakdown
- Pricing
- Guarantee

Duration - This is different from the previous template's Dates. Here you will write down 2 days, 5 days, unlimited for pre-recordings. The dates included in the first template are your plans for when you would like to do the program or when you would like to launch it or how many times per week you will advertise your program. The duration is the actual time it will take you to present the program.

Pain point & Solution - For both the Advert and Program creation, it's easier if you've already done the work on content creation, so that you can simply draw from the work you've already done.

Name & Big Promise - Write down at least 10 headliners / program names (more if you can) and again run it through the Headline Analyser. It happens sometimes that the name is too long, I then just break it down into the promise as well. For example: Join our Masterclass to make Social Media Marketing easy by using these 5 Simple Steps. Break that down into: Join our Masterclass to make Social Media Marketing easy (Name): Use these 5 Simple Steps (Promise).

Modules - What will you be discussing in your program? I recommend writing down a couple of concerns that go hand in hand with your pain point. For example, my pain point: Struggle with social media in general.

The thought that now comes to mind: Why use social media as a marketing platform in the first place? Examples of how easy it is to use the templates (using one chapter). Explain a couple of steps to boost marketing online.

Bonuses - This can range from a one-on-one call to PDFs to an eBook. Anything you can think of that you are willing to give away for free or cheaper. Go back again to your Content Creation Template for inspiration since you've already included some free offers there. You can re-use those for your program.

But here you can also add things like 30% off on your first purchase or buy now or sign-up today and get a free product / service. A bonus for a program doesn't HAVE to be absolutely free like we used for posting.

Module & Bonus Breakdown - Once you have your modules and bonuses in place, you can write down 1 or 2 bullet points underneath each one to be able to build your lesson / program content easier. Simply ask yourself these questions: What am I discussing in this module? What does my bonus template involve?

Pricing - For Paid Programs - You can have a look at your modules and create a value for each one (what you think the value is and the value to your client), including your bonuses, then add that up to get to a total.

For example:

If I chose to do a paid program and actually run you through a couple of chapters, let's say:

- Module 1 - Perfect Client (R 100)
- Module 2 - Content Creation (R 250)
- Module 3 - Creating an Advert (R 150)
- Module 4 - Build a Program (R 150)
- Module 5 - Email Automation (R 250)
- Bonus 1 - Free One-on-One call to sort out any confusion (About 30 minutes @ R 300)
- Bonus 2 - Free PDF templates of all of the above (5 Free templates @ R 70 each = R 350)

My total = R 1550
I will run this program over a 2-day period, for about an hour per session. And my goal is still to generate more clients to buy the book.

Therefore, I'll divide my total first with 2, bringing me to R775, which still seems a bit steep because I'm trying to get new clients into my general book audience. My goal is a marketing campaign. If my goal were to generate more income, I will leave it at this.

But since it's not, I divide it now by 3 which is R 517. Or dividing it by 5: R 310.

You can divide your total by any number if the total still feels too steep until you get to an amount that you feel comfortable with.

That being said and having done a million programs to get me to this point, I will happily pay R 775 compared to all the other programs available out there that usually discuss only 1 of the 5 topics I will include in this program!

When it comes to pricing, don't undervalue yourself. Too many people have too much mind drama about money. There will always be people willing to pay your price. As long as you can communicate clearly what the value will be for them. But also, do some research and see what the general market related pricing is like.

Guarantee - I don't include a guarantee for a free program, but if this was a paid program and I charged R775, I will add to my sales page or Landing Page:

MONEY BACK GUARANTEE:

If you feel that you haven't received all the tools and actionable tips to help you streamline your social media marketing by 9h00 on the day after completing the program,

I will happily refund your investment in full (subject to a 1-on-1 call to see if I can help you sort out any confusion).

Put a timeline on it, so that people don't contact you after a year and ask for their money back. Sometimes it has nothing to do with your program, but more to do with the money that they need at that moment.

You can also put things in ("Subject to") so that your client first have to "qualify" for the guarantee. It won't help, after all, if they didn't really do the work from their side.

People feel more at ease and sign-up easier if they know they can get their money back if they don't get the value that has been promised. But chances are if you know what you're doing and deliver as promised, no one will take you up on this offer.

Make your guarantee big and red and stand out on your sales page, it helps those people that are not immediate buyers make an easier decision!

Example:

PROGRAM 1

Duration:
30 Minute Video

Pain Point:
Struggle with social media in general

Solution:
Step-by-step guides to help you make it easy / simplify social media without a hassle / time saving templates included

Name:
Masterclass to make Social Media Marketing easy

Big Promise:
5 Simple Steps

Modules:
1. Why use social media as a marketing platform in the first place?
2. Examples of how easy it is to use the templates (using one chapter)
3. Step 1 – Find your Perfect Client
4. Step 2 – Profile Set-up
5. Step 3 – Create Content
6. Step 4 – Implement a Messaging Sequence
7. Step 5 – Create an Advert

Bonuses:
Perfect Client Template
Module Breakdown:

1. Why use social media as a marketing platform in the first place?
   - Social media is the best, easiest and cheapest way to reach individuals
   - There are 26.8 million Facebook users in South Africa

2. Examples of how easy it is to use the templates (using one chapter)
   - Perfect Client

3. Step 1 – Find your Perfect Client
   - Run through whole chapter

4. Step 2 – Profile Set-up
   - Explain how to insert links

5. Step 3 – Create Content
   - Explain process, what to complete first

6. Step 4 – Implement a Messaging Sequence
   - Name 5 messages in sequence

7. Step 5 – Create an Advert
   - Name 3 key elements

Bonus Breakdown:
Only 1 bonus: My Perfect Client Template PDF

Pricing:
This specific program is free

Guarantee:
For the free program I won't include a guarantee

And done!

Congratulations, you have a program!

I like to plan my advertisements for each program together with the program. I will now open my Advertising Template and make sure I'm all set to start running my program on the date that I have set as a due date.

If you have any fears that are coming up at the thought of running a program, please refer back to your subconscious and find out what it is that is causing that fear. Start with affirmations to help you change your beliefs about what you are capable of!

Client Engagement

There are so many people on LinkedIn and even more on Facebook. Yet you've seen a post from someone that might be your ideal client. Or you get a million Friend and Connection requests per day. But now what? How do you turn these people into clients?

Or better yet, your profile is stagnant. You post yes, but there's no engagement, no requests to connect with you. How do you find clients on social media?

There are a lot of businesses trying to get the attention of people scrolling through their newsfeed. What if you can make a personal connection? So that people look out for your posts and engage with you. What if you can stand out from the crowd of advertisers by using just a few simple, but different strategies?

After all, PEOPLE BUY FROM PEOPLE!

In this chapter I will give you cool tips and tricks to engage with your clients, to warm up that cold audience and to get more engagement on your posts and offers.

Most entrepreneurs will have a business page or group. It is important to turn your private personal profile into a lead generation magnet as well.

Your personal profile will be your biggest lead generation for messaging. So, keep it as professional as you would like it to be.

Now is where you start turning all those friends or connections that you don't know into clients, if they haven't yet responded to your upgraded profile.

You will be sending out your messages one-by-one. No-one said building a new business or getting new clients was going to be a breeze.

If you put in the work, you will get the results. Remember - the amount of time you spend with marketing, will be in direct correlation to the number of clients you have!

Don't use a generic program to send out multiple messages at once. People notice that very quickly and don't engage. Rather make it personal like in the following examples. An automated message sequence once got my name wrong in one of the messages. I promise you, that is not the way to attract more clients into your audience!

The messaging process is simple, but it's still a process and therefore work. Please do not feel intimidated by the amount of work that you've received from this book so far. Take it step-by-step, and you will get there. Adjust as you need to, take what you like, file what you don't, and keep on going!

CONNECTIONS / FINDING CLIENTS

Step 1

Have a look at your connection requests or friend requests.

If you receive a lot of requests:

Before just accepting everyone, have a look at each individual's profile

- Is this person your ideal client according to your Perfect Client Template?

- What do they post about? How complete is their profile? Do you see anything you don't like?

- Take the time and do this work, instead of sitting with an audience that can't help you in any way or people that post about inappropriate things that irritate you

- DO NOT be afraid to decline connection requests

- If you like someone's profile and think they might be a potential client, then accept the connection

- Send them a message immediately upon accepting (Messenger or a LinkedIn message)

Follow the message sequence in Step 2

If you don't receive a lot of connection invitations:

- Check out your friend's friends OR

- See the "Friend Suggestions" automatic feature on Facebook OR

- Search profiles using keywords

- For example: I will use keywords like entrepreneur, small business owner, online entrepreneur. Type the keyword into your Facebook search box, and tick "People" on the left. You can tick "Friends of Friends" right underneath "People" if you already have a couple of friends and would like to keep to the same kind of audience. Have a look at the profiles that come up.

- You also have the option of searching according to location, education and work under the heading "People".

- Find profiles that you think might be potential clients, that fits your Perfect Client.

- Send them a connection request, together with a message (use Messenger or LinkedIn messages)

- Follow the message sequence in Step 2

If you have friends or connections already on your personal profile, but don't know them (For existing connection):

- Go through ALL the profiles (I recommend using a spreadsheet to keep track, copy and paste the profiles that you have already checked and are happy with)
- Identify those people that might be ideal clients. If not, unfriend them or delete the connection

- If you are sitting with 500 connections and those people are not your ideal clients and you don't know them and never engage with them, then what is the point?

- Rather make your connections your audience! Use social media to your advantage as much as possible!

- And no, they DO NOT get a notification when you unfriend them. If you don't engage with each other, chances are they won't even notice.

- Once you've "cleaned up" your connections, start sending out messages.

- Use the message sequence in Step 2.

Step 2

Another way to boost engagement with potential clients, is to join groups and follow hashtags that they might be interested in.

Again, to use my example, entrepreneurs might be hanging out in groups called "Entrepreneurship", "Small Businesses", "Marketing Online" or follow hashtags with these same names.

Simply add a hashtag before the keyword to find the hashtags you are looking for. It is as simple as putting the SEARCH BOX to good use!

Once you've joined these groups and/or followed these hashtags, identify people that engage often and might be potential clients.

- Comment on their posts
- Comment on or like their comments
- Share their posts
- Ask questions
- Add valuable information on the post topic

Make yourself visible in this community!

You might find that people start approaching you! You can follow this same approach on someone's profile (depending on their security settings), comment, share or like their posts if allowed.

MESSAGE SEQUENCE

This is a summary of the messages that you will be sending out:

Message 1
Category 1 - Thank you for connecting
Category 2 - I would like to connect
Category 3 - Re-connection

Create about 5 templates (messages) that you can easily copy and paste in each of the 3 categories above, and then change them according to what you see on the person's profile.

Message 2 - Introduce what you do

Message 3 - Send free gift

Message 4 - Invitation to follow business page or group

Message 5 - Nurture

In my examples everything in brackets, CHANGES with every message.

Both Facebook AND LinkedIn will block you if you don't change it up. Don't repeat yourself too many times.

Changing part of the message every time will be fine and switching it up between the 5 messages that will be your templates to work from.

You are welcome to use my examples as your templates!

Message 1 / Category 1 - Thank you for connecting
(New connections that sent you an invitation and you accepted)

Template 1

Hi (Lucy)

Thank you for sending me a connection invite/friend request. I'm looking forward to getting to know you better and follow your success!

I see on your profile (that you like scuba diving! That must be amazing!)

(Personally, I've never been able to get enough courage together to go deeper into the sea than my knees, I'm really scared of sharks!)

Looking forward to your posts and chatting more with you.

Have a beautiful day!
(Marlize)

Template 2

Hi (Lucy)

Thank you for connecting!

I checked out your profile and saw that you (work with children. I love that! I have 2 kiddies of my own and am so passionate about a brighter future in our country.)

I'm truly excited about this connection and (sharing our passion for children.)

Wishing you a blessed day!
(Marlize)

Template 3

Hi (Lucy)

I saw some of your posts and (love your positivity!)

Thank you for sending me an invite / friend request, (I love positive posts coming up in my newsfeed.)

What do you do for a living?

Have a wonderful day!
(Marlize)

Template 4

Hi (Lucy)

Wow! I love your profile picture/ banner!

Thank you for connecting.

The old fashioned "pen-pal" just came to mind. At least we're saving on posting fees.

I would love to hear more about your (work, life and ALL your success!)

Wishing you a productive day!
(Marlize)

Template 5

Hi (Steve)

I see that you are (also an entrepreneur.)

Thank you for sending me a connection / friend request, (I love connecting with like-minded people.)

Please tell me more about what you do, (I know nothing about rigging and am passionate about learning new things!)

Have an epic day!
(Marlize)

DO NOT SELL!

The idea of this first message is to make a connection and nothing more. Keep it authentic, be a human. (I really am scared of sharks!)

Message 1 / Category 2 - I would like to connect
(New connections that you've sent an invitation to connect, directly after sending the connection request, before they accept. These messages go WITH the invitation to connect, keep them short and sweet.)

Template 1

Hi (Lucy)

I came across your profile and would like to connect with you, because (I love your valuable insights on childcare.)

Hope to hear from you soon!
(Marlize)

Template 2

Hi (Lucy)

I've been checking out new profiles to make some valuable connections and came across yours.

I think we can both benefit from this connection, (since we are both passionate about learning.)

Looking forward to getting to know you better!
(Marlize)

Template 3

Hi (Lucy)

I'm trying to connect with like-minded people on social media, since this is now the modern way of getting to know people!

Your profile grabbed my attention, because (I am also a creative person.)

I hope that we can connect and (inspire more creativity together!)
(Marlize)

Template 4

Hi (Lucy)

I've been randomly scrolling through profiles and WOW! Yours is amazing!

I love (your passion for animals that is so clear on your profile.)

I would love to connect with you and be able to re-share your posts to my connections as well!

Wishing you a beautiful day!
(Marlize)

Template 5

Hi (Lucy)

I'm building up my friends/connections list, and thought I'd sent you an invitation since we are both (into personal growth.)

I've built up a whole tribe of people for support on Facebook/LinkedIn (to help and support me with my journey and would love to hear more of your awesome advice.)

Have a wonderful day!
(Marlize)

LinkedIn

Please note that for LinkedIn you can make these messages more professional and keep the topics to what you see on each person's profile, more work related.

Also, I find that on Facebook people accept invitations very quickly and easily, so please refer back to the "Thank you for connecting" messages if they've already accepted your invites before you can get to the above message sequence.

For Facebook, you can even give it a day before sending out the above messages and only send them to people who didn't respond within that day.

For LinkedIn however, I recommend a message together with a connection request.

Message 1 / Category 3 - Re-Connection Messages
(These messages are for your current connections/friends that you've never engaged with, but might be potential clients)

Template 1

Hi (Lucy)

I realised some time ago that I have so many connections on Facebook, and yet don't know half of the people I'm friends with!

I would really like to get to know you better, since I (truly love your posts and your positivity!)

What kind of work do you do?

Wishing you a beautiful day!
(Marlize)

Template 2

Hi (Lucy)

Don't you think that it's ridiculous that we are connected on Facebook/LinkedIn and have never actually connected?

I would love to hear more about (your work and passion for colour therapy.)

Have an amazing day!
(Marlize)

Template 3

Hi (Lucy)

Do you have a lot of connections / friends on social media that you don't know?

I do! And I'm on this new mission to change that around and actually connect with the people that I'm connected to!

(How are you currently coping with life in general with all of this COVID stuff in the air?)

Looking forward to our "real" connection!
(Marlize)

Template 4

Hi (Lucy)

I saw on your profile that you post a lot (of jokes. I love that! We could all use more laughs!)

We connected some time ago but don't really know each other. Funny how social media allows us to connect with anyone in the world, and yet there's no real connection.

I would love to make this a "real" connection because (you look like someone that can make anyone laugh. I think that's a great quality to have.)

Hope to hear from you soon and chat some more!
(Marlize)

Template 5

Hi (Lucy)

Even though we don't know each other but have been connected / friends for some time now on Facebook / LinkedIn, I would like to let you know that I always see your posts come up in my news feed.

Thank you for (always being so inspirational!)

I would love to learn more about you, (what do you do for a living?)

Warmest Regards,
(Marlize)

Remember that not everyone is going to respond, and that's OK!!! Keep engaging with new potential clients and find those people that you can connect with.

There are millions of people out there, so move forward and don't fuss about the non-responders!

You are welcome to skip straight to Message 5 from here for the people who are not responding, if you would really like to make that specific connection, you can always send them a Nurture message once a month.

Message 2 - Introduce what you do

This is your second message in the sequence, and out of personal experience I've found that the people that do respond are now engaging in a proper conversation with you. Writing a message template for this section is a real challenge, because you are now responding to whatever they answered on your first message.

Responses that I've received on the first message ranges from (and I am quoting the exact messages that I've received!) "I would like to be your friend" (no "hello" or "goodbye", just this one sentence) to "Thank you for the message, but I prefer WhatsApp, here's my number…"

Your judgement will be put to the test when responding to their response. There are however those that do answer any questions asked in your first message and would like to engage.

All you do now is respond appropriately to their message and add somewhere in your message what you do (word it differently every time).

Ask another appropriate question to keep the engagement going!

The purpose of this second message is to expand brand awareness. You don't have to sell on this one yet, keep connecting with your potential client on a deeper level by just introducing what you do and getting to know them better.

All of the following examples are just snippets to give you examples but will include a "Hello" and "Goodbye" when I send them! Here are two examples:

Thank you for your kind response!

And yes, I agree, creative people should stick together.

My creativity comes out in the manner of storytelling, I write whatever I can write about that I've experienced in my own life.

I think people need more connectivity, so I try to always write as though I am speaking to you directly (and excluding all the fancy words and so on! Just having a fun conversation!)

Are you a reader?

OR

O wow, I love what you do! I think it's so cool that we are now able in our time and age to assist people with administrative tasks online. (She responded that she is a Virtual Assistant.)

My expertise lies in teaching though, I teach by telling stories of all the things that I've learned in my own life. I share my experiences in the form of books.

I'm assuming you work from home; do you find the self-discipline challenging at times?

Message 3 - Send free gift

In your third message you can share some of your knowledge. You can share a PDF, valuable knowledge, a free ticket to a webinar, etc.

You are still not selling.

Figure out what small part of your business you can share for free, without selling.

Again, respond appropriately to their response on your second message, and work your free gift into this message.

In the second example, I use someone that is going through some tough times, I just added that to show you how you can introduce your product in any situation.

Depending on what your product or service is of course, and even then, you can make a joke and say something like: how about we cheer you up with a brand-new screwdriver? You can always join our free webinar to show you how to use it to distract you for a while (Your webinar being the free gift).

I personally feel that this is not insensitive, this is my/your area of expertise and it cheers us up, right? Our passion that makes us smile. And also, I genuinely believe that some of my stories can make someone laugh!

Example:

I will definitely share your posts and spread the word on your new art lessons!

Since you are also an online entrepreneur, I would like to share with you this PDF that has made my life easier. It's how to change your profile so that your connections can see what you do and includes an automated process of how they can sign-up to whatever it is that you are offering, without you lifting a finger! (Free gift)

Try it out and see how your connections respond!

Anyway, good luck with your new venture, and I wish you massive success!!!

OR

I am truly sorry to hear about your struggles!
I would really like to cheer you up! I recorded a series for new entrepreneurs that's all about them, to inspire people to not give up! I know it's a difficult road but check out these videos. I hope you feel better!   (Insert YouTube link to pre-recorded series that I used in the content planning - All about you). (Free gift)

Do you think that you might feel better if you do something just for yourself? Learn something new and grow personally? For me that's always a good boost, to learn something new, but that's just how my brain is wired!

I wish you good luck, hang on in there and feel better soon!!!

Message 4 - Invitation to follow business page or group

This message is for if they have not already followed your page or group, because I find that once people start chatting with you, they also follow your posts more often and might have already followed your business page or joined your group.

Don't be shy to ask in the beginning of this message if they have checked out your page or group.

Your response from the previous message might already be something like: "I love your PDF!" or "Thank you for sharing the link to the video, that was awesome!" or (one that I often get) "thank you for sharing, but honestly I just don't have time".

Make sure to put all concerns to rest with this message.

If you get a "thank you, but no thank you", simply respond with "you're welcome, chat again soon" and move on to a new client.

If you've made a real connection with this person though, nurture this relationship, they might always change their mind in the future or you might still benefit in other ways from this connection, but don't spend too much energy on people that are truly not interested.

So, a typical fourth message will look something like this:

I'm so glad you liked it! How did you find the response from people when you changed your profile? Did you get any new sign-ups or inquiries?

You are also welcome to follow my business page or join my group (insert link) for cool specials and more about what I'm currently working on and making life easier for yourself! (The nerd in me comes out on the page too and I tell you all about the importance of the brain and words and how they form the way we think!)

By the way, the post you shared about the puppies this week was awesome! So funny!

OR

I'm glad you liked it!

And I get why you are concerned about the time, but this program actually helps you to save time with easy templates that you can just fill in, instead of spending hours just getting a plan together!

Why don't you follow my business page? I explain everything there, and why time is the exact opposite of being an issue, this actually saves you time! (Insert business page link)

I would love to hear your thoughts or any other concerns on this!

Message 5 - Nurture

If at all possible, try to get clients off social media as soon as possible, i.e., get an email address.

You can at any time from message 3 ask if you can rather email them some more info, or chat more via email. ALWAYS ASK PERMISSION BEFORE SENDING A TEXT OR EMAIL. If you feel the connection isn't strong enough yet, don't push this, then continue on social media up to message 5.

You can send the Nurture message once a month if you can't get in touch with this person in another way.

But if they keep responding and you've reached message 5, you can now ask them for an email address so that you can share any offers, events, or product launches via email.

This is not an effective way to grow your email list though! This is all about making new connections!

A better way to grow your email list, is to create sales pages which you should add to your business page or group for them to sign up for something. When they visit your page, because they've already had a taste of your product, the process from there should happen automatically. Please refer back to the Perfect Profile to add a link to your profile.

The idea of the nurture message is to keep in touch with potential clients that you don't have email addresses for.

Don't lose your patience with these people, some people just need more time before buying anything!

If they haven't signed up to anything yet though, here's what your fifth message will look like:

Thank you for following my business page / joining my group!

We also have cool stuff happening on email, product launches, specials and so on. (And no, I don't send out daily or weekly newsletters to irritate you!)

Would you like me to add you to the list to keep you in the loop? Please send me your email address if you are interested.

If not, you are welcome to check out our website or keep in touch via the business page.

And congratulations on your success with your big event last week!

OR

Just popping in to say hi!

Everything going well on your side?

I've recently launched a new program, which I am super excited about! Check it out here: (Link)

OR

Hope you are doing well!

How's it going with your business? I'm still going strong, hope you are too!!!

TIMELINE

Some of you might be thinking right about now that this is a shit-load of work. When on earth am I going to do all of this?

Let's have a look at the message timeline first:

Message 1 -   Directly after connection
Message 2 -   Whenever clients respond
Message 3 -   Whenever clients respond
Message 4 -   Whenever clients respond
Message 5 -   About once a month

Now the important one:

Schedule 2 to 3 days per week for engaging with clients and make these 1 to 2 hours sessions.

I engage with clients / work on social media on a Tuesday, Wednesday and Friday, for 2 hours (1 for Facebook and 1 for LinkedIn) and STOP.

Whatever I don't get to in this time, must wait for the next session. Work from the first messages sent, not the last i.e., scroll down in your messages and answer the first ones first. It's ok if you don't respond immediately!!!

Also remember that once your templates are set up, it goes easier and faster.

KEEPING TRACK

The easiest way to keep track is with a spreadsheet. I have 3 separate tabs or sheets for current connections, one for new connections that sent me an invite, and one for new connections that I sent an invitation to.

My spreadsheet looks like this, the headings running horizontally over the sheet:

- **Name**

- **Profile URL**

- **Message #1 / Re-engagement message** (Replace this message description to: Thank you for connecting or I would like to connect for the other 2 sheets) Remember: for your first message you should have the option to choose any 1 of 5 messages to send (Template Messages)

- **Yes/No / Response**

- **Message #2 / Introduction (Date Sent)**

- **Yes/No / Response**

- **Message #3 / Free gift (Date Sent)**

- **Yes/No / Response**

- **Message #4 / Invite to follow business page / Join group (Date Sent)**

- **Message #5 / Nurture (Date Sent)**

Name	Profile URL	Message 1			Message 2		Message 3	
		Template	Yes / no		Date	Yes / no	Date	Yes / no
Lucy Stevens	https://www...	Template 1	Yes		03/09	Yes	06/09	Yes
Steve Martins	https://www...	Template 4	Yes		10/09	No		

I copied my message templates into this same spreadsheet where I keep
whom. I opened new sheets or tabs for all of the different messages that

Whenever I do work on social media, I open this one spreadsheet and fin
need together in one place.

I can then immediately update my tables where I keep track. I work thro
I received, copy and paste the first message to those clients from this sa
into my "Keeping Track" table which message template I used.

I can update who has responded to my previous messages, and immediately send them the following message in the sequence, because I have everything I need right there in the same spreadsheet, separated in different tabs to easily find all the information.

Never lose sight of the goal of all of this: to make life, specifically your business processes, as simple and easy for yourself as possible!

Stop overcomplicating.
Simplify.

Email Automation

Here are the most popular beliefs about email marketing:

- Receiving too many emails gets irritating
- Automated email takes the personal touch out of communication with your clients
- It takes time to set up
- It's expensive. Or it's just another expense to get the business going

The fact is: email automation saves you an amazing amount of time and effort.

When you automate your email, you can:

- Deliver online products and services without lifting a finger
- Send emails in bulk, and not one by one by one
- Introduce your clients to upcoming launches, events and specials
- Keep in touch with all your clients
- Create sales Funnels
- Include videos in your emails

And the list goes on...

There are a lot of advantages to email automation, and to address the above-mentioned concerns:

- No, you don't have to send out 3 emails per day. You can time the emails anyway you like. Personally, an email to keep touch and touch base once a month is fine for me (excluding any special emails or product sales).

- You can still add a personal touch to your emails, you are writing them after all. Simply keep them authentic and chat to your clients as you would in a "normal" email.

- Yes, it takes time to set up. But once it is set up, the work is done!

- MailChimp (which we will be discussing) has a free plan for your first 2000 contacts. If you have more than 2000 contacts, you should be able to pay for their upgraded plan or take a serious look at your email list!

Please also keep in mind that when you use MailChimp, you don't only have to automate your emails.

You can send a once-off email for a product launch or special. The advantage of using MailChimp for this purpose though, is that you already have your populated email list that includes tags, so that you can send emails to a specific set of people (one of your Perfect Clients).

What can you use automated emails for?

1. Grow your email list using a Landing Page
2. Monthly Mailer / Newsletter to keep in touch and nurture your audience
3. Once off email for an event, launch or special
4. Sales Funnels to warm up your audience before selling your product
5. Direct product selling, again using a Landing Page

We will run through creating a Landing Page and Email, (Once Off or Sequence) step-by-step in this chapter.

There are a lot of buttons to click, so please work through this chapter at your own pace, especially if you think you are not a technical guru. But all you need to do is follow the steps and have your email set-up in no time!

Please also note that this being another software program it does change as they upgrade their systems. The basics of how it works stays the same though, even if the interface (what you see on the screen) might look different.

All examples will again be for this book, but please adjust your names and tags and headings to fit your business.

Before we get started...

CREATE A MAILCHIMP ACCOUNT

1. Use this link to open a free account: https://mailchimp.com/

2. Simply pick the Free Plan option to get started.

3. You can only create 1 audience, which is no problem at all. You will differentiate between clients using tags.

POPULATE YOUR EMAIL LIST / CONTACTS

If you have an existing audience somewhere on a spreadsheet, you need to import these contacts:

1. Save your spreadsheet as a CSV file

2. In Excel, you will "Save As" a CSV file

3. In Google Sheets, you will "Download" as CSV file

4. Go to Mailchimp and make sure you are on your dashboard page. That is the page you see when you go into your Mailchimp account, with the menu on the left.

5. Select "Audience" on the left, and then "All Contacts"

6. Click "Add Contacts" and then "Import Contacts"

7. Select "Upload File" and "Continue to upload"

8. Browse and select your CSV file

9. Click "Continue to organise"

10. Under status, select "Subscribed"

11. Click "Continue to tag"

12. Your next step is to create a tag - this can be anything from: "Existing Clients" / "Nurture" / "2020" - tag these contacts with whatever word you like, so that you know who they are. (In my work, I tag contacts with my book titles or nurture)

13. You can create more than 1 tag for a contact if you like

14. Once your audience is tagged, click "Continue to match"

15. On the next page you will see all the columns that appear on your CSV / spreadsheet. (If there is a red column with an exclamation mark, click on it and resolve the issue by using the suggested criteria that they give you for the column.)

16. Select or deselect all the columns that you would like to import: Name, email, phone number, etc.

17. Then click "Finalise import"

18. Make sure that you have no more than 2000 clients listed in this document to continue with the free plan, click "Complete Import"

19.   This is a rather quick process, but depends on how many clients you have listed

20.   When the import is done, you can now view your contacts in your audience tab under "All contacts."

You can use this process for ANY list with emails that you currently have. If you have email addresses from a previous job, you can tag these emails with "New", because these contacts don't know about your current business venture.

For them, create emails that will introduce them to your product or service, before starting to sell anything! Explain to them that your path has taken a different route and what you now do and why this is your passion.

Keep in mind that if you have emails from a previous company, you might also have Restraint of Trade on any and all of their clients. Please make sure that you are allowed to contact these clients again before doing so.

You might also get requests to unsubscribe someone from your list, simply go to this person in your Audience, click on their name, and unsubscribe them, without taking any offence!

If you don't have an existing audience but would like to grow your email list, I suggest:

- Create an advert with a FREE product / service that you can offer your clients to grow your email list. Your free product or service can be anything from doing a live Facebook training, pre-recorded videos, a PDF document, or one-on-one call with the client. Go back to your Content Planner and have a look at what service or product you can offer for free. Or build a new program specifically for this purpose.

- Create a landing page and add the link of your landing page in your Advert (We'll run through Landing Pages just now!)

- Your audience that signs up for the free product will enter their name and email on the Landing Page, and automatically appear in your contacts tab.

- With Mailchimp, you no longer have to ask people to drop their emails for you in the comments of a post, rather have them fill in the landing page to make this process automatic.

- You can also build a Funnel (using TheWebpreneur), which I explain in the Funnels Chapter, for the same purpose of growing your email list.

Step 1 - Create a Landing Page

A Landing Page is a single webpage that appears in response to a link that is clicked. A typical Landing Page will contain all the benefits of why you should subscribe or buy a product or service, a guarantee for purchase, an introduction for your company and ALWAYS a "Subscribe" or "Buy Now" or "Get my Free Product" button (CTA).

A Landing Page is best described as a single webpage that sums up an entire website or a service or product. We use Landing Pages to convince clients of what they will get out of buying your product or subscribing to your program. The advantage of using a Landing Page, instead of referring people to a website, is that there are no distractions. There is a list of benefits or product description, and a single button that the client should click.

You can design a Landing Page however you like. It can be a short "A4" page, or a much longer page that your clients have to scroll down to read. You can design it with bright colours, or highlight important statements, or make lists, or even include pictures and images of yourself or your products. When you create a Landing Page, have that Perfect Client of yours in mind, and create it according to the look that you would like your brand to have.

A Landing page is typically only one page, on MailChimp we use it for this benefit and clients give you their details. With a Funnel we create more than one webpage.

Create your first Landing Page:

1. Go to your MailChimp dashboard, select "Create" on the menu on the left. (That is the blue circle with the pencil icon.)

2. Scroll down and select "Landing Page".

3. Name your Landing Page - The clients will not see this name, so make it anything that will make sense to you: "Grow my list" / "New clients" / "Free service" / "Facebook audience" - whatever you like.

4. Your audience will always be the same, like I mentioned before with the free plan you can create only 1 audience (if you have more than one business, you can still separate your clients using tags) and select "Begin".

5. Now select a template - Selecting a template is really not that important, since you can edit this as much as you like once you get started. Also note that they will let you know if you are not allowed to use a template according to your payment plan - For the purpose of this exercise, I will select "Grow Your List".

6. Now you can edit your Landing Page:
    a. All editing happens on the right-hand side, your preview is on the left.
    b. You can click on any "block" on the preview (the page that you are building) and an edit block will appear on your right.
    c. You can now edit all your blocks according to "Content", "Style" and "Settings" on your right.
    d. NOTE THAT THERE ARE 2 "SAVE AND CLOSE" OPTIONS. DO NOT press the one at the bottom right (the blue button) until you are happy with your preview. You must select the "Save and Close" button just above the one at the very bottom, that is inside your block, to continue with editing the next block.

e. The best thing to do here is press all the buttons that you can press, click on all the blocks in your preview, play around with fonts, colours, add an image or logo, make it bigger or smaller and under "settings" move it left, right or centre, and familiarise yourself with the editing functions.

f. REMEMBER TO SAVE AND CLOSE each block when you are happy with that block!

g. You can edit the button where people will "sign-up" as well: change the colour or text ("sign-up", "get my free product", "deliver to my inbox now"), see the preview after sign-up, etc

7. Adding a block:

a. Once you've pressed "Save and Close" for a block, you will see all the options for more blocks on your right

b. Drop and drag blocks into your template (Text, Boxed text, Divider, or even add a video if you like).

c. On your preview, when you hover the cursor over a block, you will see an arrow at the top of each block. Use this arrow to move your blocks up and down on your preview by holding the arrow and dragging the block up or down.

d. Edit your blocks by clicking the pencil icon that also comes up if you hold your cursor over each block.

e. You can add benefits to your Landing Page, all the reasons why people should sign up for your product or service or otherwise customise your Landing Page as much as you like.

    f.   In the block where people have to fill in their details, keep it as simple as possible! DO NOT let them complete an entire page with info. Don't even ask for a surname or telephone number, just a name and email will be enough.

8. When you are happy with your Landing Page you can select the "Save and Close" button at the very bottom of the page, the BLUE "Save and Close" button.

9. The next page will include all the details for your Landing Page. This is where you select a tag for the audience that will be signing up via this specific Landing Page.

10. Select "Edit Audience"

11. Tag your new members and save. OR create a new tag by selecting the + button. Simply type in your tag and click on the tag (the text)

12. At the top right, you can now "Publish" your Landing Page.

13. Back on your Dashboard, under Campaigns (the megaphone icon), you can now view your Landing Page as well as the link that you can copy and paste into your Social Media posts.

14. There is also a report you can view, to see how many people have viewed or visited or signed up using this Landing Page.

15. Again, all the clients that have signed up can be viewed under Audience, with the different tags that you have created.

You can use your Landing Page on social media, in emails, on phone messages or wherever you like! You now have the link. Whenever someone clicks on this link, your Landing Page will come up, no matter what device they are using or which platform.

This is the first step to automate business processes, but don't be overwhelmed by thinking that you have to create a whole webpage by yourself, make it as simple as you like it to be!

Step 2 - Create an email

You can now either deliver your free product or service (training video, PDF, info for program) to your client's inbox with a once off email, or create an email sequence to upsell, tell your client more about your company, etc.

To create a once-off email is the first step in the email sequence, but I will show you how to create more than one email:

1. Again select "Create" on your left-hand-side menu on your Dashboard.

2. Select "Email".

3. At the top of the next window, you have 3 options: Regular, Automated and Plain-Text.

4. Select "Automated" and then "Email Subscribers When They're Tagged".

5. Add your campaign name and select "Begin".

6. Now you can edit your trigger. (Leave the other 3 options as they are)

7. Select when you would like this first email to go to your clients. Usually, the first email goes out immediately after a client has signed up. You can even create 2 emails that go out immediately after a client has signed up, a Welcome email and the other with the info/ product/ service, etc. The second email can then go out the following day (1 Day after they are tagged), the third email 2 or 3 days after they are tagged, and so on.

8. Select the tag as well for this group of audience that you would like to send this specific email to.

9. Select "Update Trigger"

10. And then "Design Email".

11. Fill in the form on the next page.

12. The "Preview Text" is optional (I usually leave this blank and only include a subject).

13. The "From Name" is what your clients will see who the email is from. You can for example change this to your

business name or Marlize- Author, instead of just your name.

14. If you have more than one email, you can go back to your Dashboard and add the emails in your Account settings in MailChimp and choose which one to use under "From Email Address".

15. Click "Next".

16. Select a Template.

17. Edit and create your email (using the same guidelines as previously described for the Landing Page.)

18. To add a PDF, drop and drag the "Button" block into your email.

19. Under "Link To" select file and upload your PDF into Mailchimp.

20. To add a video, add the "Video" block to your email and copy and paste your video URL from either YouTube or Vimeo.

21. When you are happy with your email, before selecting the blue and final "Save and Continue", select the "Preview and Test" at the top of the page and send yourself a test email.

22. If everything looks good, you can click the blue "Save and Continue" at the bottom of the page.

23. Confirm that you are ready to send your email by clicking "Next".

24. And lastly, "Start Sending".

25. Your email will now start going out automatically to all the new clients that subscribe on your Landing Page.

26. To create a sequence, follow this same process, only change your trigger for WHEN every email should go out to your clients (as described above under point number 7).

27. Everything that you create can be viewed in the Campaign section.

You might notice in your left menu on the Dashboard that there is an option for Automation. To use this option, you need to upgrade your plan. By creating your emails using triggers is a perfect solution for any start-up business, and also makes it easier for you to familiarise yourself with MailChimp functions before upgrading to a paid plan.

You will now be able to successfully set up Landing Pages and send out automatic emails without sitting in front of the computer for an entire day!

Email Automation

Funnels

Please note that there are a lot of different names for Funnels, including Sales Funnels, Click Funnels, Product Funnels and so on. For the purpose of simplicity and to not confuse these Funnels with the Email Funnels discussed in the previous chapter, I will refer to these Funnels as Sales Funnels.

Where a Landing Page consists of only one webpage, a Sales Funnel will have multiple webpages, each with a clear button that you can click to continue to the next page.

Think of the shape of a funnel, a typical kitchen funnel that you use to pour liquid into a bottle with a small opening. The top is wide, and the bottom becomes narrower, to allow the liquid to go into the bottle without spilling.

This is exactly what the function of a Sales Funnel is. Initially, you will have a hundred people clicking your link to enter the Funnel. About 70% will continue to click the button on the first page. 50% of people will actually fill in the form to subscribe or buy on the second page, and only 30% of people will follow through and click the last link that you might add to up-sell a product or service.

In effect, you are thinning out the crowd, and finding your Perfect Clients. Those that are truly interested in your product or service, allowing you to populate your email list with real clients or even potential clients, and not with people that will unsubscribe within a week.

A Landing Page can be used to generate email addresses, leading to an Email Funnel where you can sell (whether that may be a product, a program, a PDF, a service, etc.). In comparison, a Sales Funnel does not rely on emails to sell, but rather includes all the steps for a sale right there and then. Sure, the product, service or information to a program can still be delivered via email, but the sale has already happened by the time you reach email.

That being said, you are welcome to create a Funnel for a free product, service or program as well. I find Funnels more reliable, since you don't have to depend on someone opening a chain of emails. The free "sale" then still happens on the Funnel pages, and only the end product is delivered to an inbox via email.

A Sales Funnel can be anything from 3 to 7 pages long. Typically, your first page (the page that appears when someone clicked on your link), will list all the benefits of a product or service, a guarantee and/or an introduction to yourself or your company. You can add a video presentation or images. But ALWAYS, add a button that reads "Subscribe now", "Buy Now", "Sign Me Up", or however you choose to word it.

Your second page will include the form for people to fill in their details TOGETHER WITH a payment option. For payments, you are going to have to research and see what works for you and your company, and also depending in which country you are located. In South Africa, PayFast is an easy way to go. Here you do not want to include EFT, because there is no automatic process that will confirm payment into your bank account, to be able to continue with the next step in the Funnel.

Remember that the idea of a Funnel is to automate sales. After you have created the Funnel, everything should happen automatically.

After the "Checkout" in your Funnel, you can either add an up-sale or a down-sale on your Thank You page. An up-sale will be for example: "Click here to upgrade your product/service" OR "Get this special offer with your purchase that is valid only on this sale" (or for a limited time) OR anything else that you can sell with your original sale.

A down-sale is when someone decides to not go through with the sale after all, and you add an extra page where a discount is available. You can either do this on your original product, or on the extra product or service you were using as an up-sale.

As complicated as all of this sounds, going through the process of creating a Funnel is simple with today's step-by-step websites to help you along the way.

Create a Funnel:

After a lot of research, especially regarding pricing, I have found a website that offers an affordable and easy way for you to create a Sales Funnel: The Webpreneur (a link to this website is included in the Resources section.) When it comes to Sales Funnels, there are unfortunately no free options available.

The first thing you will have to do is to create an account and choose a payment option. Once your payment has been processed, you will be able to enter your dashboard. From there, you can go to Builder and start building your Funnel.

The Webpreneur offers multiple, beautiful and 100% customisable templates, and easy step-by-step guides to get your Funnel set up the way you want to.

Two other big advantages of working through this website, are that you can add a custom domain and link your Funnel to MailChimp. Which means that all the client information that is added to your Funnel, will automatically go to MailChimp, where you can add tags and send out emails automatically as well. The Webpreneur also offers excellent support, should you need any help setting up your Funnel.

You can add images, change colours, add or remove blocks or even add a countdown timer for a specific offer. They help you to track the amount of clicks your link has received, how many people have viewed your page and view all your new clients that have signed up.

In Summary

Instead of relying on people to open their email for you to make a sale, you can create a Sales Funnel that will take a client through the steps of purchase from one page to the next, without any delay or days in between.

A Sales Funnel will take a client from one page to the next immediately, by just clicking the "next" button on every page.

You can then use email to deliver a product or service, send out nurture emails or newsletters, or inform clients of special offers and events taking place, instead of trying to sell on email. Sales Funnels help you to generate immediate sales, without you lifting a finger.

Funnels

Templates

This chapter serves as a summary and includes all the templates that have been mentioned throughout this book.

You can copy these tables into your own spreadsheets and have them ready to be edited!

There are a couple of templates that work well in PDF format. You can create them either in a document program, or in a spreadsheet. I like to print these out, paste them in a book and write out the information in pencil, instead of using the computer.

The templates that work well in A4 PDF are:

- Perfect Client
- Advertisement
- Program
- Article

For Content Creation and the Messaging Sequence, I would recommend creating and using spreadsheets in Excel or Google Sheets.

However, you choose to use the templates, remember to make them work for you!

Perfect Client

Age	
Gender	
Marital Status	
Experience / Education	
Job title / Function	
Finances	
Industry	
Region / Country / Province	
Languages	
One sentence that describes them	
Values	
What are their desires/needs?	
Describe an average day	
Which basic human need are you addressing? (Certainty / Significance / Connection / Growth)	
Before Sale	
Emotions	
Challenges	
Objections to sale	
After Sale	
Emotions	
Challenges	
Objections to sale	
Can you save your ideal client time or money?	
Groups	
Hashtags	
Keywords	
Activity	

Advertisement

Planning	
Niche	
Goal	
Paid/Free	
Recurring	
Duration / Post Dates	
Where?	
Number of Adverts	
CTA	
Funnel	
Email Action	
Advert 1	
Type	
Pain Point	
Solution	
Headliner	
Big Promise	
Guarantee	
Copy	
Image / Video	
Results / Engagement	
Re-Run 1	
What am I changing?	
Results / Engagement	
Re-Run 2	
What am I changing?	
Results / Engagement	

Program

Planning	
Program Dates	
Niche	
Goal	
Paid / Free	
Recurring	
Where / How?	
How many people can attend?	
Time	
CTA	
Email Action	
Program 1	
Duration	
Pain Point	
Solution	
Name	
Big Promise	
Modules	
Bonuses	
Module Breakdown	
Bonus Breakdown	
Pricing	
Guarantee	

Article

Topic:	
Name/ Headline:	
Personal Background / What do I have to do with it?	
Why are you doing this?	
What's your passion?	
Topic Background:	
Who am I talking to?	
Pain Points:	
How do they feel? Think about emotions	
Solutions / Benefits:	
What will they have gained after purchase?	
How will you solve their problem?	
Can you save them time and/or money?	
Pros and cons:	
Science:	
Leaders in your industry:	
My product / My thoughts:	
What makes you unique?	

Content Creation

Table broken up according to space. These headings should all be next to each other, running horizontally over the spreadsheet.

Pain Point, Struggle, Concern and Objection	Benefits/Solutions in general

Benefits/Solutions specific to your product / service	Who am I Talking to?

Podcasts / TED Talks / Video Clips	URL

Articles	URL

Leaders in Your Industry / Science / Statistics	Free Content

Holidays and Other Special Days	What else can I write about?

Why am I doing this?	

Content Creation - Sequence

Table broken up according to space. These headings should all be next to each other, running horizontally over the spreadsheet.

Pain Point:	Name of sequence:

Post/Video # 1:	Post/Video # 2:

Post/Video # 3:	Post/Video # 4:

Content Creation – Monthly Planner

	Week 1	Week 2	Week 3	Week 4
Monday				
Tuesday				
Wednesday				
Thursday				
Friday				
Saturday				
Sunday				

Content Creation – Content Planner

Table broken up according to space. These headings should all be next to each other, running horizontally over the spreadsheet.

Day	Date	Goal	Type	Pain Point	Topic

Content	Hashtags	Image	CTA

Where am I posting?	Engagement

Client Engagement – Keeping Track

(Message Sequence)

Table broken up according to space. These headings should all be next to each other, running horizontally over the spreadsheet.

Name	Profile URL	Message #1 Re-engagement message	Yes / No Response

Message #2 Introduction	Yes / No Response	Message #3 Free gift	Yes / No Response

Message #4	Message #5
Invite to follow business page / Join group	Nurture

Client Engagement – Templates

Message 1 / Category 1 - Thank you for connecting

Template 1
Hi (Lucy)
Thank you for sending me a connection invite/friend request. I'm looking forward to getting to know you better and follow your success!
I see on your profile (that you like scuba diving! That must be amazing!)
(Personally, I've never been able to get enough courage together to go deeper into the sea than my knees, I'm really scared of sharks!)
Looking forward to your posts and chatting more with you.
Have a beautiful day!
(Marlize)

Template 2
Hi (Lucy) Thank you for connecting! I checked out your profile and saw that you (work with children. I love that! I have 2 kiddies of my own and am so passionate about a brighter future in our country.) I'm truly excited about this connection and (sharing our passion for children.) Wishing you a blessed day! (Marlize)

Template 3
Hi (Lucy) I saw some of your posts and (love your positivity!) Thank you for sending me an invite / friend request, (I love positive posts coming up in my newsfeed.) What do you do for a living? Have a wonderful day! (Marlize)

Template 4
Hi (Lucy) Wow! I love your profile picture/ banner! Thank you for connecting. The old fashioned "pen-pal" just came to mind. At least we're saving on posting fees. I would love to hear more about your (work, life and ALL your success!) Wishing you a productive day! (Marlize)

Template 5

Hi (Steve)

I see that you are (also an entrepreneur.)

Thank you for sending me a connection / friend request, (I love connecting with like-minded people.)

Please tell me more about what you do, (I know nothing about rigging and am passionate about learning new things!)

Have an epic day!

(Marlize)

Client Engagement – Templates (Continued)

Message 1 / Category 2 - I would like to connect

Template 1

Hi (Lucy)

I came across your profile and would like to connect with you, because (I love your valuable insights on childcare.)

Hope to hear from you soon!

(Marlize)

Template 2

Hi (Lucy)

I've been checking out new profiles to make some valuable connections and came across yours.

I think we can both benefit from this connection, (since we are both passionate about learning.)

Looking forward to getting to know you better!

(Marlize)

Template 3
Hi (Lucy) I'm trying to connect with like-minded people on social media, since this is now the modern way of getting to know people! Your profile grabbed my attention, because (I am also a creative person.) I hope that we can connect and (inspire more creativity together!) (Marlize)

Template 4
Hi (Lucy) I've been randomly scrolling through profiles and WOW! Yours is amazing! I love (your passion for animals that is so clear on your profile.) I would love to connect with you and be able to re-share your posts to my connections as well! Wishing you a beautiful day! (Marlize)

Template 5
Hi (Lucy) I'm building up my friends/connections list, and thought I'd sent you an invitation since we are both (into personal growth.) I've built up a whole tribe of people for support on Facebook/LinkedIn (to help and support me with my journey and would love to hear more of your awesome advice.) Have a wonderful day! (Marlize)

Client Engagement – Templates (Continued)

Message 1 / Category 3 - Re-Connection Messages

Template 1
Hi (Lucy) I realised some time ago that I have so many connections on Facebook, and yet don't know half of the people I'm friends with! I would really like to get to know you better, since I (truly love your posts and your positivity!) What kind of work do you do? Wishing you a beautiful day! (Marlize)

Template 2
Hi (Lucy) Don't you think that it's ridiculous that we are connected on Facebook/LinkedIn and have never actually connected? I would love to hear more about (your work and passion for colour therapy.) Have an amazing day! (Marlize

Template 3
Hi (Lucy) Do you have a lot of connections / friends on social media that you don't know? I do! And I'm on this new mission to change that around and actually connect with the people that I'm connected to! (How are you currently coping with life in general with all of this COVID stuff in the air?) Looking forward to our "real" connection! (Marlize)

Template 4
Hi (Lucy) I saw on your profile that you post a lot (of jokes. I love that! We could all use more laughs!) We connected some time ago but don't really know each other. Funny how social media allows us to connect with anyone in the world, and yet there's no real connection. I would love to make this a "real" connection because (you look like someone that can make anyone laugh. I think that's a great quality to have.) Hope to hear from you soon and chat some more! (Marlize)

Template 5
Hi (Lucy) Even though we don't know each other but have been connected / friends for some time now on Facebook / LinkedIn, I would like to let you know that I always see your posts come up in my news feed. Thank you for (always being so inspirational!) I would love to learn more about you, (what do you do for a living?) Warmest Regards, (Marlize)

Templates

Resources

For free high-quality images use Unsplash:
https://unsplash.com/

Create memes, banners, adverts, and video clip adverts with Canva:
https://www.canva.com/join/macho-invest-line

Unicode Text Converter help you to "bold" your headliner, or make it italic for any post:
http://qaz.wtf/u/convert.cgi?text=Oh%2C+the+Places+You%27ll+Go%21http://qaz.wtf/u/convert.cgi?text=Oh%2C+the+Places+You%27ll+Go%21

Run your headliners through Headline Analyzer to test them:
https://www.aminstitute.com/headline/

Build sales funnels with Thewebpreneur, merge with Mailchimp and Payfast:
https://thewebpreneur.tech/a/vvmakn

Use Mailchimp for email marketing, automation and keeping in touch with your clients:
https://mailchimp.com/

www.ingramcontent.com/pod-product-compliance
Lightning Source LLC
Chambersburg PA
CBHW071552200326

41519CB00021BB/6718